CUBA

A Guide for Cruise Passengers

Richard Detrich

Photos, unless otherwise noted, are by the author or are historical images believed to be in the public domain, U.S. government photos and illustrations, or products of employees working for the U.S. government.

Contents

Introduction

It always bugged me that although I was a citizen of the United States of America, the home of the brave and land of the free, for political reasons I was not free to visit our next-door neighbor, Cuba. Maybe in part because it was forbidden, Cuba has always fascinated me. But it wasn't just that it was the forbidden fruit. Here was this country just 90 miles [145 kilometers] offshore that had such a fascinating culture and history! Even in the early days of European exploration of the "New World," Cuba was the key to exploration of much of the Americas.

So, when U.S. President Barack Obama first announced a softening of travel restrictions on ordinary U.S. citizens going to Cuba, I was eager and began reading everything I could get ahold of about Cuba. I was determined to be on board the first cruise ships authorized by the U.S. to take U.S. people to visit Cuba.

The first ship to go was FATHOM, formerly the old ROYAL PRINCESS, a ship that I loved. FATHOM was a short-lived effort by Carnival Corporation that failed, not because of Cuba, but because it was such an ill-conceived concept that combined a somewhat superior do-gooder program of an essentially ineffective type of "community service," with a 60s type of touchy-feely, sit around and sing "Kum By Ya," type of onboard programming. The 60s were great in the 60s but didn't translate well into cruising in the 21st Century.

The second company in was tiny Pearl Seas Cruises, a one ship operation run by the much larger American Cruise Lines. I missed the first sailing, but I was on the second, and have been on every voyage since. And I fell in love, not just with Cuba, but with small ship cruising as well.

My challenge as a destination consultant and speaker on board ships is to provide guests with background and information that will help them get the most out of their voyage and their time ashore. I've been doing this now for ten years and I've noticed that some guests take the time before their cruise to read and research the places they will visit. I've seen folks who put together loose-leaf briefing books on their research that would put a White House briefing book to shame. And I've also seen guests who plunk down good money to take a cruise and get on board without a clue where they are going. Like the two gals from the U.S., both in their 60s, who were walking out of the theater on this huge ship after my talk about the Panama Canal. I overheard one gal say to the other, "I didn't know the Panama Canal was man-made." Well, at least I had cleared that up!

Because the Cuba cruises for U.S. guests by current U.S. law cannot be cruise "vacations," but must be people to people educational adventures, my talks about Cuba's background, history and culture, and my "Take 15" talks about the next day's port of call, are an important and welcome part of the onboard experience.

The folks I typically meet on board small ships bound for Cuba are well-read, well-educated, well-traveled people, with amazing life experiences, and are eager to soak up everything they can about the places they are visiting. They love Cuba, meeting the Cuban people, experiencing the different cultural and artistic encounters ashore, reveling in the architecture, and of course, loving all those old "Yank Tank" cars.

I do not pretend to be an expert, historian, or authority on Cuba. I am a communicator, a presenter if you will, a lecturer who tries to distill a whole lot of information into a presentation that will help ordinary travelers get the most out of their visit to Cuba.

Often, people will ask, "Richard, do you have a copy of that talk?"

Well, yes, I do ... and here it is! Expanded a bit, but here it is.

Richard Detrich

Cuba 101[1]

People, if you dig down beneath all the exteriors, are pretty much the same the world over ... they have the same needs, fears, aspirations ... but how they process all that, and how their lives develop, and the social and political impacts, are different. So, in that sense people *are* different ... and their ideologies are different. Societies are different. Governments are different. Expectations are different. Our task as world travelers is to experience, to listen, and to learn. If you do that you will thoroughly enjoy and love the people of Cuba, you will be enriched, and have a wonderful time. The Cuban people are warm, welcoming, and eager to interact with their American neighbors from the U.S.

Although the people aren't always the first thing folks think of when they think "Cuba."

Many folks think first of the old classic cars. These old American cars from the 50s are locally called Yank Tanks and many are used as taxi cabs. Those that are freshly painted and restored are used primarily as taxi cabs for tourists. And the old, ancient looking, but still running, ones are used as taxi cabs for locals. Don't worry: you will see them! It's estimated there are around 60,000 of these still on the road in Cuba, about 35% of the cars in Cuba. So, you can't miss them!

Because of the 1962 U.S. Embargo, Cuba could not import new cars from the U.S., nor parts for the existing cars. Cuban ingenuity keeps these old cars running! However, to keep the cars running most have been modified often with replacement Soviet or Chinese diesel engines. So mechanically they are anything but original parts. Those fancy chrome fenders and decorative items can't be imported so they are fabricated in Cuba using just pieces of old steel and very primitive metal working tools, only working off photos of the original cars.

Of course, you think of Cuban rum. Sugar and rum production have played an important part in Cuba's history. What most Americans think of as "Cuban" rum is Bacardi, which originated in Cuba and during U.S. prohibition fueled rum smuggling. Eventually, when after the Revolution everything was nationalized, Bacardi fled to Florida and Puerto Rico, and now is owned by a giant French distillery. Since the Revolution a rum called Santiago is produced at the old Bacardi distillery in Santiago de Cuba. You can buy Cuban rum for around $7 a bottle and the price is fixed by the government so you don't have to shop around for the best deal.

Even if you're a nonsmoker, you think of Cuban cigars. Cigars were used by the Indigenous Taino in Cuba when Columbus arrived. Tobacco use was taken back to Europe where it was thought to have therapeutic qualities by some, while others believed it had demonic effects on the user ... a little like what some folks today think about pot. But tobacco cultivation and rolling cigars have always been a major aspect of Cuban life and commerce.

A lot of us think of Cuba in terms of Barry Manilow's song "Copacabana" ... about Lola, a showgirl in a mythical nightclub "the hottest spot north of Havana." However, the song was inspired not by a nightclub in Cuba, but the real Copacabana Hotel in Rio de Janeiro, which is considerably South, not North of Havana. And although there is a Hotel Ipanema and nightclub in Havana, "The Girl from Ipanema" is also about Brazil. But

A Yank Tank in Cienfuegos.

Cigar smokers' heaven: Cuba cigar shop.

both songs inspire dreams and thoughts about a maybe pre-revolutionary Cuba.

I've had a number of folks say, and I've thought this myself, "I need to get to Cuba before, like China, it's all changed. Before Havana becomes a giant cruise ship parking lot like Nassau." Well, sorry Charlie ... Cuba has been open to foreign tourists since 1980 ... U.S. Americans are the late arrivals to the party!

Canadians and Europeans have been enjoying Cuba for 35 years! Cuba gets 2.6 million foreign tourists per year, before the change in U.S. policy, and although we won't see it, foreign investments from Canada and Europe have been building resorts and tourist infrastructure. Because, by U.S. law, trips for U.S. citizens must be "educational" and the U.S. Treasury Department definition of "educational" does not include laying on the beach under swaying palm trees, sipping mojitos and watching beautiful bodies go walking by in skimpy bathing suits.

There is a certain mystery about Cuba because for most of our lives, and for some of us all our lives, at least for U.S. Americans, Cuba has been off-limits. North Americans generally don't know much about the history of other regions or countries, even that of our next-door neighbors. So many of us in the U.S. haven't known a lot about Cuba.

What is amazing is that since the Revolution, against all odds, Cuba has made remarkable changes and achievements. The man who was the founder of a free Cuba, Jose Marti, Cuba's national hero, said that the only way to be free was to be educated. Education is prized, and many folks are highly educated, but often doing jobs which don't really take advantage of their education. Education is free to all from nursery through university and is mandatory through the ninth grade, so almost everyone is literate.

Home ownership, a major tweak in the original Marxist revolutionary theology is claimed to be greater in Cuba than in the U.S. ... so they say. And unemployment in Cuba is supposedly lower than in the U.S. But having been there, I'm not sure how they are counting. Most Cuba watchers have little confidence in figures produced by the Cuban government.

There is home ownership, but many people rent, not own, or live in what is essentially a tiny corner of a building their family owned but they have no money to maintain the property, so they live in an improvised section of the building, almost like squatters in their own properties. And there seem to be a lot of people who are unemployed, certainly underemployed given my observations. You'll discover in Cuba, as in almost all countries, things aren't always what they seem to be or what they pretend to be or what people would like to think they are. Just like in every country there is a "party line" which does not always reflect reality.

Since 1991 Cuba has been a secular state rather than atheist state. One no longer must be an atheist to be part of the ruling Communist party. Cuba has always had two major religions, Roman Catholicism and religions originally brought by slaves from Africa. What you have in Cuba today is the strange melding of aspects from traditional Christianity with traditional African spiritualism. Most who practice these traditional African religions are also baptized Roman Catholics. During slave days the slaves were able to hide their traditional religions in plain site by cloaking them in elements of the slave owner's Christian religion. Religion in Cuba has many layers and things are not always what they appear to be on the surface. We'll talk about this in a later chapter.

A lot of us look at Cuba as a backward country, somewhat Third World, because they drive old classic cars, which would be worth a fortune in the U.S., and they lack our consumer mentality, largely because of the Embargo by the U.S. and the collapse of the Soviet Union which had pumped massive support into Cuba.

A Yank Tank owner/operator can make in a single hour more than a physician makes in a month.

Street music is a way of life in Cuba, like these guys in Trinidad.

Sometimes we get stuck in the past in our thinking, or just assume that every other country must be inferior to our own country, whatever country that is.

Cuba is a regional leader in medicine and has sent doctors as volunteers or as professionals paid by the countries that hire them all over the world. In the latter case they are hired by the Cuban government and sent abroad providing a major revenue source for the Cuban government[2]. Cuba has 6.7 doctors per 1,000 people vs 2.5 doctors per 1,000 in the States. Medical care is free for Cubans. Cuba has the lowest infant mortality and the highest life expectancy in Latin America.

In 2015 Cuba managed what the World Health Organization called "one of the greatest public health achievements possible," eradicating mother-to-child transmission of HIV and syphilis. However, the average Cuban doctor, or teacher for that matter, makes the equivalent of $30 U.S. *per month*! A specialist maybe up to $60 U.S. per month! So, in many cases your guide in Cuba may be trained as a doctor but can make far more as a tour guide. A lot of this, quite frankly, is because of the U.S. Embargo. There is what the average Cuban calls the "tourist apartheid" in Cuba. There are the regular Cuban hospitals for ordinary Cubans, and other hospitals that are only for tourists and government officials.

 A U.S. friend who has family that he regularly visits in Cuba, tells me that if you go to a typical Cuban hospital you will likely have excellent personal care by a well-trained doctor, but you need to bring your own sheets, toilet paper and light bulbs since these are in short supply due to the U.S. Embargo. Needles need to be reused in Cuba, a fact of life that makes most people cringe.

On one sailing we had several retired radiologists sailing with us, and they managed to get into one of the hospitals. They said, "Richard, you wouldn't believe what they have to work with. They are struggling to use equipment that was old back when we graduated from medical school."

Things are not always what they seem in Cuba. You are going to eat well when you are off the ship. As a tourist you are going to eat far better than most Cubans.

For example, cows are regulated by the government. Even if it's your cow, you can't slaughter it without a permit from the government because the cows are needed to provide milk for children. Adults don't drink milk. You may well have lunch ashore featuring local shrimp, lobster or beef ... these are rarely available or affordable for most Cubans. So, it is important to know when visiting Cuba, as really in ANY country, that things are not always what they seem.

Cuba is the largest island in the Caribbean, and, excluding continents, the 17th largest island in the world, just smaller than the U.S. state of Pennsylvania. It has 11 million people with a median age of 40, higher than most Caribbean nations. 64% of the population are white, 26% mestizo or mixed, and 10% black.

Governmentally, Cuba might be described as a work in progress as it attempts to successfully blend Marxist-Leninist socialism with the realities of an interconnected, global, capitalist economy. Fidel retired to the role of senior statesman and is now dead. Raul Castro, has been President and pretty much has been the political power, but he is planning to retire.

At this writing, it is an open question what happens next, which we will talk more about in a moment. There is an elected National Assembly of People's Power that meets twice a year pretty much to approve executive decisions of the President. All 614 elected members are all members of the Cuban Communist party.

This is far from an open society. Call it what you will, but Cuba has been, and is, a military dictatorship. Raul Castro has power because he is the head of the military evidenced by the fact that at key moments, or when making important policy statements to the Cuban people, he always appears in his military uniform.

Originally the island was inhabited by Taino Arawak people. In October 1492 Columbus arrived and claimed the island for Spain. We don't know what Columbus looked like, although you'll find lots of artists images of Columbus. It is believed that he had red hair, fair skin, and a ruddy complexion from all his days at sea. We do know what he wrote in his journals, journals which are now on display at the General Archive of The West Indies in Seville, Spain. About Cuba, Columbus wrote, "Never have I seen anything so beautiful, full of trees that line the river, beautiful and green with their flowers and fruit, countless fowl and birds that sing sweetly."

Columbus didn't "discover" Cuba because, like all the New World places he visited, the local Indigenous knew who they were and where they lived!

The first Spanish settlement was at Baracoa in 1511, and Havana was settled in 1515. The Indigenous people who were here when Columbus came were virtually wiped out, not just by the harshness and oppression of the Spanish settlers, but by diseases for which the locals had no immunity.

I find it fascinating is that in 1549 when Gonzalo Perez de Angelo was appointed governor, he understood the Spanish threat to the Taino people and culture, and immediately declared the liberty of remaining natives, something in which Cuba was way ahead of other Spanish colonies

Cuba developed slowly but importantly as an urbanized society that primarily supported the Spanish colonial empire. Because of its geographic position and its importance in the Spanish colonial empire, Cuba became known as the "key" to the Caribbean which obviously made it a target of the other major world powers all vying for a piece of the action in the New World. Cuba became the major rendezvous point for the Spanish

Treasure Fleet in route from Panama and Columbia to Spain. The fleet would stop in well-fortified places like Havana and Santiago de Cuba, and San Juan in Puerto Rico, to take on water and provisions before hoping on the Gulf Stream, a kind of 101 ocean freeway, back to Spain.

There ae some spectacular and wonderfully preserved historic forts in Cuba, like the El Morro Castle in Havana, and the spectacular fort we will see as we sail into Santiago de Cuba. These forts were built to defend Cuba from all the major sea powers of the day that were competing to seize control of the West Indies. Spain had to fight them all off to keep control of Cuba which, because of its location, was the key to the Caribbean. Cuba lived in constant fear of attack not just by the warships of competing countries, but from attack by pirates, or sanctioned thieves known as privateers like the Englishman privateer Francis Drake, and the Dutchman Piet Heyn who successfully plundered the Spanish fleet in Havana harbor

As the Seven Years War in Europe spilled into the Caribbean, in 1762, the British seized Havana and Cuba. But their occupation was short lived because in 1763 the Treaty of Paris, ending the Seven Years War, gave Cuba back to Spain in exchange for giving Florida to the British. Yet. in less than one year of British rule, Cuba was changed dramatically. Trade was introduced between Cuba and North America and other islands in the Caribbean. Most importantly, the British developed the sugar industry which would dominate Cuban life. To provide labor for the sugar industry the British began importing slaves and eventually major U.S. companies would develop huge sugar plantations and supporting industries in Cuba.

Colonial Cuba developed two very different, and very unequal societies. The landowners who grew cotton, tobacco and sugar grew wealthy on the backs of poor slaves. As sugar became more and more lucrative, the sugar elite grew more wealthy and powerful. In Cienfuegos and Trinidad are magnificent mansions which were just the second homes of those who profited from sugar. This basic inequality would simmer, and still simmers, throughout Cuba's history.

Eventually most of the Indigenous people died off, the Spanish settlers came, and Cuba became a very prosperous Spanish colony. Still today, everywhere you look in Cuba you will see evidence of the Spanish culture and influence in all the beautiful Spanish architecture. Still very evident is the idea of the Spanish plaza surrounded by the city, the plaza being the center of life, gossip, friendship, commerce, and even romance. That was the beautiful side of being a Spanish colony. But Spain became more and more demanding, repressive and oppressive so by the mid-19th Century Cubans were getting restless and wanted Independence from Spain. Simon Bolivar, the Great Liberator of Latin America was successfully leading the countries of Latin America to independence from Spain, and the Caribbean island of Cuba longed for the same independence.

U.S. Americans were captivated by their neighbor's fight for independence from far-off Spain. The poet Jose Marti, who was living in exile in the U.S., lobbied for the U.S. to get in the war and the popular press echoed his sentiment for the U.S. to join in Cuba's fight for independence. For one thing, by this time vast amounts of U.S. money had been invested in Cuban industries like sugar, chocolate and railroads, and U.S. American economic interests saw a potentially burgeoning opportunity if Cuba were independent from Spain.

One of the most famous and beloved Cubans to ever live was Jose Marti, often called "The Apostle of the Cuban Revolution." Marti is one of the most beloved Cubans to ever have lived and is revered as a national hero. He was born in Havana in 1853 and was a poet and patriot. A strong advocate of independence from Spain, he was first exiled in 1871 and spent much of his time abroad working as a diplomat for other Latin American countries. He lived in New York City for a while, actually in the Bronx. There is a statue of him on horseback in Central Park.

In 1895 Marti returned to Cuba to fight for its independence. But he was a poet and not a soldier. He died on the battlefield fighting for Cuban independence from Spain in 1895 at the age of 42. His most famous quote, and the basis for Cuba's policy of free education for all from preschool through university is, "People can only be free if they are truly educated."

Eventually slaves became more and more expensive to import, either legally or illegally, and sugar became more expensive to produce. Then when the world price of sugar crashed, and plantation owners were forced to look for outside help.

Outside investors, largely from the U.S., invested heavily in the Cuba sugar business, often buying huge plantations at distressed prices, granting loans at high interest. They also brought the technology of the day, ways to produce sugar more efficiently and even built railroads to conveniently transfer product to the ports.

Havana was a world-class city in the late 1800s with a population greater than that of New York City. There was serious discussion in the U.S. about annexing Cuba to the U.S. by one way or another, and a U.S. invasion of Cuba was actively talked about until the U.S. Civil War. A continuing option was possible statehood for this island just 90 miles [145 kilometers] off the U.S. coast.

Although Marti died long before Castro's revolution, he saw the dangers of switching one group of folks living high off the hog on the backs of the poor, for another, even if called socialism. He said, "Socialist ideology, like so many others, has two main dangers. One stems from confused and incomplete readings of foreign texts, and the other from the arrogance and hidden rage of those who, in order to climb up in the world, pretend to be frantic defenders of the helpless so as to have shoulders on which to stand." Most of the monuments to Marti since the 1959 Revolution don't include this quote.

The Jose Marti Memorial in Havana is located on the northern side of the Plaza de la Revolucion and consists of a 3,589-foot or 109-meter tower in the form of a five-pointed star made of grey marble from the Isle of Pines, today known as Isla de La Juventud. A competition was held for the design of the monument, but when Batista seized power in a coup in 1953 he rushed to complete the project ignoring the winning design for one that he preferred, one that had placed third in the contest. The memorial was completed in 1958 and consists of a giant statue of Marti, a museum, and a tower visible as you sail into Havana harbor. Today tours stop at the memorial, not so much to honor Marti as to ogle the collection of old cars there eager to take tourists around town for an hour for more than a typical Cuban doctor makes in a month!

You will see another monument and statue of Jose Marti when we get to Cienfuegos, and almost every town in Cuba has some monument to Marti.

Among U.S. Americans, Marti is probably best known for the words of a poem, which were partially adapted to the text of the song *"Guantanamera."* The version popularized by folk singer Pete Seeger is the one most familiar to North Americans.

> *I am a truthful man,*
> *From the land of the palm.*
> *Before dying, I want to*
> *Share these poems of my soul.*
>
> *My verses are light green,*
> *But they are also flaming red.*
> *My verses are like a wounded fawn,*
> *Seeking refuge in the mountain.*
>
> *I cultivate a white rose*
> *In June and in January*
> *For the sincere friend*
> *Who gives me his hand.*

And for the cruel one who would tear out
This heart with which I live.
I cultivate neither thistles nor nettles
I cultivate a white rose.

I know about a fatal evil
Among the unspeakable shames:
The enslavement of human beings
Is the great shame of the world!

With the poor people of this earth,
I want to share my lot.
With the poor people of this earth,
I want to share my lot.
The little streams of the mountains
Please me more than the sea.

Outside investors, largely from the U.S., invested heavily in the Cuba sugar business, often buying huge plantations at distressed prices, granting loans at high interest, and they brought with them the technology of the day, ways to produce sugar more efficiently and even built railroads to conveniently transfer product to the ports.

Havana was a world-class city in the late 1800s with a population greater than that of New York City. There was serious discussion in the U.S. about annexing Cuba to the U.S. by one way or another, and a U.S. invasion of Cuba was actively talked about until the U.S. Civil War. A continuing option was possible statehood for this island just 90 miles [145 kilometers] off the U.S. coast.

If on your free time people to people exploration you choose to walk about 15 minutes from the dock in Cienfuegos to the center of town, you will pass by the resting place for old steam locomotives, quietly rusting away. These old engines played a very important part in Cuba's history and in her relationship with the U.S., as the U.S. kept pouring investment into the island.

El Morro Fort in Havana.

El Morro Fort in Santiago de Cuba.

As Cubans fought for Independence from Spain, there was pressure in Washington and in the popular press in the U.S. to protect "U.S. Interests" in Cuba. The "U.S. interests" were not people, not U.S. citizens or Cuban people, but all the major companies that had invested in Cuba.

In 1898 as Cuba was struggling to throw off Spanish rule and become independent, the U.S. sent the 6,000- ton battleship MAINE to Cuba to "protect American interests" i.e. American companies and investment in Cuba. On February 15 the MAINE exploded killing 260 crew members. To this day nobody knows for certain how the ship exploded, quite possibly it was an explosion of ordinance improperly stored in the ship, but it was quickly attributed to sabotage by the Spanish and this idea was heavily promoted in newspapers that favored the U.S. jumping into war with Spain.

The rallying cry for entering the war with Spain became, "remember the MAINE, to Hell with Spain."

An interesting sidelight is that the nearest U.S. battleship was the OREGON in San Francisco, and to bring the ship 16,000 miles [26,000 kilometers] around the Horn to Cuba took 66 days, nor incidentally highlighting the U.S. military need for a canal across Central America.

Interestingly along the Malecon, that famous seaside promenade in Havana, the U.S. erected an imposing monument to the victims of the MAINE. It featured two classic Greek columns with a giant American eagle at the top. After the failed Bay of Pigs Invasion, the American eagle was ripped from the monument and the memorial plaque was replaced by one that now reads, "To the victims of the Maine, who were sacrificed by imperialist greed in its eagerness to seize the island of Cuba."

The Spanish-Cuban-American War lasted just over three months and was fought in Cuba, Puerto Rico, Guam and the Philippines.

During the war an Assistant Secretary of the Navy named Theodore Roosevelt resigned to serve with the Rough Riders, gaining national fame that later led to his being chosen as running mate for William McKinley. When McKinley was assassinated, Theodore Roosevelt at 42-years-of-age became the youngest President of the United States in history [Kennedy was 43, Obama 47].

In 1898 the Treaty of Paris was signed between the U.S. and Spain ending the war and granting the United States its first overseas empire with the ceding of such former Spanish possessions as Puerto Rico, Guam, and the Philippines.

Representatives of the former Spanish possessions were not included in the discussion.

Many viewed this as a power grab by the U.S. To put all this in perspective, at the time empire building was what all the great nations did! England, France, Portugal, Belgium, Germany were all intent on building empires, and no one did this better than the British who, at the height of the British Empire, controlled 25% of the earth's surface. Five years earlier the U.S. had thrown out the queen and annexed Hawaii. Now it added Cuba, Puerto Rico, Guan and the Philippines to its growing empire.

To keep all this in order, Roosevelt needed a strong navy, and to keep that navy strong he needed a path between the seas. He tried to convince Colombia, of which Panama was part, on the idea of the U.S. building a canal across the Isthmus of Panama. When that failed, the U.S. simply encouraged Panamanian dissidents to declare independence from Colombia. The U.S. then agreed with a non-Panamanian, a Frenchman named Bunau-Varilla, to turn over to the U.S. a swath of land across the newly hatched "Banana Republic" of Panama in order to build a canal, thus giving the U.S. another colony in its crown, the U.S. Panama Canal Zone.

In Cuba the U.S. just took over running Cuba as its colony, since it had won the war and the island. It appointed as governor a former general in the Confederate Army, Fitzhugh Lee, to run Cuba. Yes, he was the nephew of *that* General Lee. So, a man who might well have been tried for treason against the U.S., who had repeatedly gone into battle to preserve slavery, was made governor of the American-occupied colony of Cuba. Another early ruler of occupied Cuba was General Leonard Wood, after whom the fort in Missouri is named. Wood was an army surgeon who worked his way into being first appointed as governor of the Philippines, and then Cuba.

The U.S. ran the show and controlled everything and unofficially ran a policy of segregation with power and prestige for the whites. Blacks were looked upon as an unfortunate remnant of slavery, and, as was the law in the U.S. at the time [Plessy v. Ferguson 1896], one drop of black blood made you black.

Cuba had been freed from one oppressor only to be taken over by another. Jose Marti, based on his time living in exile in the U.S. wrote, ""It is my duty to prevent, through the independence of Cuba, the U.S.A. from spreading over the West Indies and falling with added weight upon other lands of Our America. All I have done up to now and shall do hereafter is to that end . . . I know the Monster, because I have lived in its lair--and my weapon is only the slingshot of David."

Money and investment from the U.S. poured into Cuba. European and American capital controlled most of the industries in Cuba. The U.S. invested heavily in infrastructure and modernizing the sugar industry with railroads and improved processing facilities. Guantanamo became a key coaling station for U.S. ships in the Caribbean. But most ordinary Cubans were left out still without freedom and independence.

As the U.S. built its growing empire, it sought to create in Cuba a model for countries which had a certain aura of independence, yet remained firmly controlled by the U.S. The U.S. agreed to remove U.S. troops and control from Cuba only after Cuba agreed to something called the Platt Amendment. This was an amendment tacked onto a 1901 Army appropriation bill by a Senator named Orville H. Platt that has proven to be a plague haunting U.S. and Cuba relations ever since. The Platt Amendment said the U.S. would leave Cuba only if Cuba agreed to the Platt Amendment which had two onerous terms. The U.S. had the right to intervene unilaterally in Cuban affairs, and the U.S. had the right to a Naval base in Guantanamo.

Reluctantly Cuba signed on, and that began a history of "independence" characterized by failed governments, violence, bloodshed, revolution, military coups, dictatorships, and politicians eager to line their pockets with government resources.

When people think of a Cuban dictator, supported and propped up by the U.S., they usually think of Batista. And when they think of a U.S. president visiting Cuba, they often think just of Obama. Although Obama is hands-down still the most popular U.S. politician/celebrity to get to Cuba, two sitting presidents have visited Cuba including Barak Obama and Calvin Coolidge. Jimmy Carter visited as a former president. Franklin Roosevelt and Harry Truman visited the US Navy Base at Guantanamo Bay, Cuba and not Cuba.

When Obama visited, what stunned the Cuban people was to see Obama walking the streets of Old Havana along with his wife AND his mother-in-law. By law, Cubans know virtually nothing about the family and personal lives of their leaders. Here was the President of the United States walking down the streets of Havana with his wife. And, in a country where multiple generations often share the same living quarters, to have his mother-in-law walking alongside was particularly endearing to Cubans.

Cartoon from the day

Cuban Capitol built 1929 intentionally to loosely resemble U.S. Capitol

---

RichardDetrich.com

The first Cuban dictator supported and endorsed by the U.S. was not Batista, but Geraldo Machado, a former cattle thief turned politician. He was authoritarian and an admirer of Mussolini. The night before the visit of U.S. President Calvin Coolidge, Machado had four Communists, a Spaniard, a Pole, and two Cuban students, arrested for putting up anti-imperialist posters. No sooner had Coolidge left than a fisherman caught a shark that had human remains inside. It was all that was left of the Spaniard and the man's wife was able to identify his cufflinks, after which she was promptly deported. The four had been dumped off El Morro castle, possibly alive, or dead ... Machado responded by blaming the sharks and banning shark fishing.

By 1933, with the country was in chaos and ready to collapse into anarchy, the U.S. decided it could no longer support the dictator Machado. He and his supporters, including the father of musician/actor Desi Arnaz, fled the country.

In 1933 during political confusion and turmoil, an Army sergeant named Fulgencio Batista was part of a bloodless coup and seized control. Batista quickly promoted himself to colonel and later made himself chief of the armed forces. As such he controlled a string of puppet presidents. In 1940 he had himself elected President of Cuba on a populist platform. He instated the relatively progressive 1940 Constitution of Cuba and served until 1944. After finishing his term, he lived in Florida, then returned to Cuba to run for president in 1952. Facing certain electoral defeat, he led a military coup preempting the election.

In his second term Batista did not continue his progressive social policies but focused on creating his own fortune. He became an absolute dictator executing an estimated 20,000 Cubans and imprisoning others. The bagmen from Mob-run casinos nightly delivered to Batista bags of cash, his share of the day's take, from 10 to 30%. The U.S. continued meddling in Cuban affairs supporting various governments and dictators when they cooperated with U.S. political and economic interests.

Prohibition in the U.S. was a highly profitable for Cuban tourism and rum runners. Organized crime flourished and influenced the Dictator Batista who was also supported by U.S. But there was growing dissatisfaction with Batista in Cuba as well as by the U.S.

In the 50s as the Cold War geared up, the Senator from Wisconsin, Joseph McCarthy, fueled fears of Communist subversion in the U.S., of an advancing "Red Tide" that threatened to destroy everything U.S. Americans held dear ... And in searching for subversives McCarthy did manage to challenge many of the things U.S. Americans did hold dear. Even today, when many people in the U.S. think of Cuba, they think of fear of "Communism," somehow fearing that tiny little Cuba might be able to do what the combined efforts of Viet Nam, the People's Republic of China, and the Soviet Union combined could not do!

Unfortunately, the U.S., in response to what it viewed as the Communist threat of a red tide sweeping over the world, chose to back and finance the worst dictators of Latin America, some of whom attended the U.S. Army School of The Americas in the Panama Canal Zone. Men like Batista, Samosa, Pinochet, and Noriega, all dictators, were enemies of the people, enemies of freedom, really enemies of the things the U.S. holds dear, but unfortunately the U.S. has had a long history of backing the wrong pony. But as Franklin D. Roosevelt once said of the dictator Samosa when he was oppressing the people of Nicaragua and his Secretary of State told FDR that Samosa was a "bastard," FDR summed up U.S. foreign policy by saying, "He may be a bastard, but he's our bastard."

If you want to read more about this sordid tale of U.S. support of some of the worst Latin American dictators, do a Google search on "CIA Operation Condor" - like the bird) and read the official U.S. government material released under the Freedom of Information Act. It is a sad and disturbing history which,

"Our man in Havana" - Cuban Dictator Fulgencio Batista with U.S. Army Chief of Staff Malin Craig in Washington, DC

Batista's soldiers executing a rebel by firing squad in 1956

although we may not like it, we need to know about to stop making the same mistakes.

Batista, although admittedly a bastard, was the U.S. man in Havana and he protected the interests and investments of U.S. companies and was in league and in the pockets of the Mob who ran the big tourist hotels and casinos. He represented those who had money and power in Cuba. He was "*our* bastard."

Interestingly, when John F. Kennedy was a junior senator he was "entertained" by the Mob in Havana complete with a fully staffed "party" room equipped with beautiful women. The mobsters were too dumb back then to film the action, and this was before the private lives and sexual improprieties of politicians and celebrities were the daily lead stories on TV news and the Internet. So, we will never know, thankfully, what went on behind closed doors.

When he became President, John F. Kennedy's advisor Arthur Schlesinger, Jr observed, long before the Castro Revolution, "The corruption of the Government, the brutality of the police, the government's indifference to the needs of the people for education, medical care, housing, for social justice and economic justice ... is an open invitation to revolution."

That "invitation to revolution" was accepted in 1952 by a brilliant young lawyer named Fidel Castro who was running for election to the Chamber of Representatives. He circulated a petition to depose Batista's government which was ignored and that began a seven-year struggle to overthrow the Batista dictatorship. Fidel was joined by his brother Raul and later by a young Argentine Marxist medical doctor named Che Guevara and they launched a revolutionary guerilla war.

One of Castro's first audacious actions was to attack the giant Moncada army barracks Santiago. It's now a museum and school which sometimes, but not always, is pointed out by the guides

The "Red Scare" of the 50s

Many powerful U.S. companies, including the Mob, had a vested interest in Cuba

in Santiago de Cuba as we drive by. But it is of enormous historical significance in Cuba. Castro had organized a group with the purpose of toppling Batista. One of Castro's fellow plotters was an employee of an American sugar refinery and another was an accountant with General Motors, but most of the cadre were just ordinary workers and farmers. They planned to attack the Moncado barracks to capture weapons with which to arm their movement and provoke a popular uprising. To overcome the overwhelming numbers against them, they planned their attack for July 26, forever enshrined as 26 de Julio, the evening of the first day of Cuba's Carnival celebration, anticipating that the soldiers would be too wasted to resist.

Nothing worked out as expected because someone had tipped off Batista's soldiers. Only a few of Castro's men were killed in the actual attack but 68 were captured, tortured and later executed. Of those who survived, 32 ended up in prison, and another 50 escaped.

Fidel escaped initially but was later captured and taken to prison. The Army Lieutenant who captured him did not approve of the torture that was taking place at Moncada Barracks, so he took Castro to the civil prison in Santiago. Had Fidel been taken to the Moncada Barracks it is unlikely he would have survived. That, plus the spotlight of the local media, likely saved Castro from torture and death.

Castro ended up imprisoned in the notorious Presidio Modelo, or Island Prison which was a massive state-of-the-art prison when it was built, modeled after one in Joliet, Illinois. The prison had four gigantic round cell blocks. Guards were kept in an observation tower in the center so that guards and prisoners never had any contact. After the Revolution Castro changed the name from Isle of Pines to Isla de la Juventud and the prison was turned into a museum. Near the entrance to the first cell block is cell 3859 where Castro was in prison for two years in solitary confinement. From his prison cell Castro wrote many letters and planned how to use propaganda and the media as tools of his revolutionary movement, and he wrote his famous defense plea, "History will absolve me."

While he was in prison, awaiting trial, the lawyer Castro prepared his defense, and when he finally had his day in court he gave the court a four-hour speech in his defense. It was a very lawyerly speech, more like a law school lecture than the fiery speech of a rebel defending of his actions. It was controlled, measured, and legally academic, the kind of speech judges would understand. Castro said, "To those who would call me a dreamer, I quote the words of Jose Marti, 'A true man does not seek the path where advantage lies, but rather, the path where duty lies, and this is the only practical man, whose dream of today will be the law of tomorrow, because he who has looked back on the upheavals of history and has seen civilizations going up in flames, crying out in bloody struggle, throughout the centuries, knows that the future well-being of man, without exception, lies on the side of the duty.'"

After four hours Castro concluded, "I know that imprisonment will be as hard for me as it has ever been for anyone--filled with cowardly threats and wicked torture. But I do not fear prison, just as I do not fear the fury of the miserable tyrant who snuffed life out of 70 brothers of mine. *Condemn me. It does not matter. History will absolve me.*" The entire speech was quickly printed up into a pamphlet which became a very effective propaganda tool.

In 1954 Batista stepped down from the Presidency he had seized to legitimately campaign to be officially elected President. Naturally, since he already controlled the island, he ran without opposition and ... guess what! He was elected and assumed office. To celebrate what he believed was the "legitimacy" of his election and feeling in control and all-powerful, and with a visit by U.S. Vice President Richard Nixon giving credibility to his legitimacy, Batista granted a general amnesty to all prisoners. Guess who walked out of prison on the isle of Pines in May 1955?

Out of prison, the Castro brothers got out of Cuba while the getting out was good and headed off to Mexico, where they met a young Argentine revolutionary, trained as a doctor but who never practiced, by the name of Ernesto "Che" Guevara. Together they organized the 26th of July Movement, named for the date of the unsuccessful attack on the Moncada Army Barracks, with the goal of overthrowing Batista.

They planned and plotted in Mexico and then Fidel led a group of 82 fighters to Cuba aboard an overloaded, leaky old yacht nicknamed "Granma," now immortalized in Cuban history landing in the eastern part of Cuba. Planned uprisings by the July 26 Movement in Cuba to divert attention had failed, and when they landed they were ambushed by Batista's troops who had been tipped off to the landing and were waiting. Castro and 11 others escaped into the mountains of Sierra Maestra.

From prison Castro had written many letters and planned how to use propaganda and the media as tools of his revolutionary movement. When the Batista news outlets were reporting that Castro had been killed during the ambush of the Granma landing, Castro arranged for a reporter from the New York Times to visit with him in the mountains and take a series of carefully staged pictures which created the image of Castro as a modern-day Robin Hood fighting for the rights of the oppressed. The pictures helped dispel the rumor that Castro had been killed. Here was proof that he was alive and there was hope for the people of Cuba to topple the dictator, if necessary, by force.

Fidel's father, Angel Castro Argiz, immigrated to Cuba from Spain and eventually had a sugar plantation, was relatively well-off and the Castro's enjoyed a comfortable life. His mother was Lina Ruz Gonzales. Fidel attended private boarding school, and then Belen College, a Jesuit high school where he was obsessed, like most Cubans, with the national sport of baseball, and he dreamed of becoming a professional ball player.

Fidel studied law at the University of Havana. His sense of injustice and rebelliousness found a target at university. Castro threw himself into student politics and was distraught when he failed to become head of the students' federation. The political action groups at the University operated like political gangs. Castro would later comment that has four years at the University were more dangerous than all the time he fought against Batista in the Sierra Maestra mountains. It was during this time that Castro gained national attention with a charismatic speech criticizing government corruption.

A guy by the name of Eduardo Rene Chibas Ribas was Castro's mentor in national politics. Chibas was a popular radio personality who was the "nation's conscience."

Chibas warned that Batista might attempt a military coup and promised evidence to that effect. When the congressman who had promised the evidence to Chibas refused to present it, to save face and apologize, Chibas shot himself live on his radio show. Unfortunately, his timing was off and at the moment he dramatically shot himself they had gone to a commercial message and the whole effect was lost. He died of his self-inflicted wound, but his popular socialist message of social justice and fighting corruption made a lasting impression on Fidel.

In 1952 Fidel Castro was a young lawyer running for a seat in the Chamber of Representatives and he circulated a petition to depose Batista's government claiming it had illegitimately suspended the electoral process to steal the Presidential election for Batista. The courts did not act on the petition and ignored Castro's legal challenges making it clear to Fidel that armed force would be necessary to get Batista out. That began a seven-year struggle to overthrow the Batista dictatorship. Fidel was joined by his brother Raul and later by the young Argentine Marxist medical doctor named Che Guevara.

The Castro Family Album

Long before Donald Trump came down the escalator in Trump Tower to announce that he was running for President, Castro figured out how to build an image and a brand and effectively milk that image and use the media to get what he wanted. The young lawyer Castro carefully created and managed the image of a Robin Hood revolutionary fighting the rich oppressors and to liberate his people. He invited well-known journalists, reporters, and photographers to his guerilla camp and gave interviews and staged pictures to create the image. A parade of media celebrities made their way to interview Castro including Edward R. Murrow and Barbara Walters. Even Gina Lollobrigida managed to get an assignment from an Italian magazine to interview Fidel.

On one cruise I met a passenger who had been on the VIP detail of NYPD when Castro visited the United Nations. Castro would always leave his hotel suite dressed in fatigues and was careful in restaurants to always order fried chicken, eat with his hands, and throw the bones on the floor, all to maintain the image he had carefully crafted.

Many were impressed by the logic and goals of the Revolution, including Kennedy who said, "I believe that there is no country in the world including any and all the countries under colonial domination, where economic colonization, humiliation and exploitation were worse than in Cuba, in part owing to my country's policies during the Batista regime. I approved the proclamation which Fidel Castro made in the Sierra Maestra, when he justifiably called for justice and especially yearned to rid Cuba of corruption. I will even go further: to some extent it is as though Batista was the incarnation of a number of sins on the part of the United States." Of course, that rather enthusiastic opinion was open to change.

In 1959 the dictator Batista, with U.S. urging, left the country voluntarily, and Fidel marched into Havana and took over. It had been six years since that first attack on the Moncada Barracks in Santiago de Cuba. Even his entry into Havana, like everything else, was a carefully timed and staged event. The rebel forces, poised to claim victory, hung out just outside Havana until Fidel arrived from the other end of the island to lead a triumphant entry.

Within months of taking control, Castro moved to consolidate his power by brutally marginalizing other resistance groups and figures and imprisoning and executing opponents and dissident former supporters. As the revolution became more radical and continued its persecution of those who did not agree with its direction, thousands of Cubans fled the island, eventually forming large exile communities abroad, particularly in Florida.

Almost immediately the properties of those who had fled, and all those U.S. interests and big companies were nationalized. In Havana you don't want to miss the magnificent art deco old Bacardi headquarters building, today home to offices of government functionaries. If you can get the guard to let you into the lobby, you will still find the distinctive Bacardi bat symbol on the door and elevator plates.

Faced with oppression, threats of imprisonment and torture, singled out for being reeducated because they were intellectuals, artists who didn't fit the political mold, religious, gay or just didn't follow the party line, thousands of people left behind everything and risked their lives to find freedom. There are two very famous movies that reflect the struggles of people deciding to leave their homeland, both of which are available on YouTube, "Before Night Falls" and "Strawberry and Chocolate."

Castro had established himself as a political brand, but it wasn't easy being Castro. He ruthlessly consolidated his power making enemies within and without, which of course helped create more enemies. Those who had relatives killed, who lost everything, who fled Cuba, of course hated Castro.

When he seized U.S. assets he quickly became enemy number one and the symbol of the feared "red tide" of Communism that had come to the U.S. doorstep. Castro's security people claimed there were 741 assassination attempts on Castro, mostly by the CIA including at one time enlisting a former lover, working for the CIA. She was, to stick a poison pill in Fidel's drink, but at the last minute she couldn't do it, and her story, told and retold, has proved very profitable.

Its far easier to proclaim a new society than to create one. Cuba knew it needed a strong ally if it wanted to create a Marxist socialist society on the doorstep of the U.S. and needed a benefactor nation that could provide this tiny, now even more impoverished nation with financial aid. The two obvious choices were both Cold War foes of the U.S., the Soviet Union and the People's Republic of China. Unfortunately, Cuba had to choose. Che may have found China to be more Marxist, but ultimately Cuba aligned with the Soviet Union.

Already suffering from the U.S. Embargo and having experienced the failed Bay of Pigs Invasion, Cuba lived in fear of its giant neighbor to the North and Kennedy had long forgotten his optimistic assessment of Castro back when Castro was hiding out in the Sierra Madre Mountains. More and more, Castro rightly saw the U.S. as his enemy and the Soviet Union as more than willing to provide protection

To put things into perspective . . . In 1959 Castro marches victorious into Havana, a new government is formed and things, including assets of U.S. corporations, are nationalized. In 1960 Eisenhower puts an Embargo on Cuba and early 1961 breaks relations. In 1961 there is the ill-conceived disaster of the Bay of Pigs Invasion, followed almost immediately by the Cuban Missile Crisis. Those of us who were alive at that time can remember Kennedy's speech the night the crisis came to a head, wondering if we would wake up the next morning or be consumed in a nuclear holocaust. The Blockade of Cuba eventually morphed into an Embargo, a version of which is still in effect over 50 years later. Thus, began the long history of neighbors in conflict with one another.

Cuba became very dependent for its existence on its partner, the Soviet Union. Then for Cuba the unthinkable happened. The Soviet Union, on which Cuba had become so dependent, collapsed. If it was difficult before, it was even worse now. Cuba found itself in desperate economic straights and thus entered what Castro called "The Special Period" which demanded great sacrifice.

There were wide-spread shortages of food, frequent electrical outages, and civil disorder. Then Cuba was struck by three hurricanes in a row, adding to the problems, leaving 200,000 homeless, and over $5 billion U.S. in property damage. Cuba developed relationships with Venezuela, which of course ended up with problems of its own. Fidel resigned, and Raul became president. Adjustments were made in the economy including currency reform, allowing foreign investment and limited free enterprise.

One of the most stunning moments in history for me was when Richard Nixon, of all people, went to China, opening relations and business with one of the staunchest Communist countries. China is now one of our major trading partners and a major investor in the U.S. We are even friends with Viet Nam. So, the time had come!

President Obama, announcing the reset of U.S. Cuba policy, said, "Neither the American, nor Cuban people are well served by a rigid policy that is rooted in events that took place before most of us were born ... After all, these 50 years have shown that isolation has not worked. It's time for a new approach ... Today, America chooses to cut loose the shackles of the past so as to reach for a better future –- for the Cuban people, for the American people, for our entire hemisphere, and for the world."

Sometimes there comes a time in national life and history when you need to hit the reset button.

The current President of Cuba is Raul Castro, Fidel's younger brother, who was with Fidel from the beginning. Raul is now 86 and as of this writing planning to retire in 2018, probably taking the role of senior statesman. And then there is the memory of Fidel, one of the most influential figures in the history most of us lived and certainly the most important in Cuba.

Fidel's Triumphant Entry into Havana

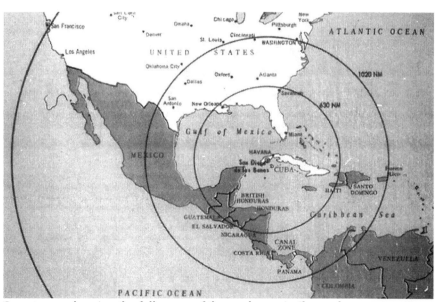
Secret map showing the full range of the nuclear missiles under construction in Cuba, used during Cuban crisis.

When we think of Fidel, we have in our minds the heroic black and white images of Fidel the revolutionary with his beard and cigar. In his heart of hearts, I think Fidel was mostly a socialist and a true communist with a small "c." Then, I think, influenced by Che, and perhaps Raul, and for pragmatic reasons he embraced a more hard-core Marxist-Leninist approach. Then, after the Revolution, he discovered power and wealth, and had a life that was considerably different, and far better than that of his people. With Castro's death it will be interesting to see what happens. With new leadership and direction in both Cuba and the U.S., big questions loom.

My sense is that while Cubans are grateful for Fidel and his contributions, that the popularity of the Castro family with ordinary Cuban people and even the military, has been slipping. The median age in Cuba is 40, older than you'd expect in the Caribbean, but remember, many of those who left after the Revolution were young enough to endure the journey and start their lives over. My sense is that the younger generation in Cuba is ready for change and ready to be part of the rest of the world.

A controlled press in Cuba means for Fidel Castro that details of his family and private lives, including details of any indiscretions, cannot be revealed or discussed. But we know he had two marriages, a half-dozen relationships, some of which produced children, so it appears that Fidel was somewhat of a "player" and that perhaps being a celebrity maybe left him feeling that he had the right to . . . well, you know.

In retirement, Fidel and his second wife lived well, certainly far better than most Cubans, but also far less luxurious than what most people would expect for someone of his fame and stature. Because of all the assassination attempts, they lived in a heavily guarded military compound. Again, because of assassination attempts, all his food was grown within his compound and prepared by carefully watched military chefs.

In 2006 Fidel underwent surgery for intestinal bleeding, a risky procedure that ended up being botched, and as a result his health deteriorated even more. He delegated his presidential duties to his brother Raul, and as his health continued to decline. in 2008 he announced his retirement and assumed the role of elder statesman, meeting with popes and visiting dignitaries.

Even in his old age, Castro demonstrated that he hadn't lost any of his fire. After Obama's trip to Cuba, with whom Castro did not meet, Castro wrote in his newspaper column, "Cuba has no need of gifts" from the United States, saying "Our efforts will be legal and peaceful, because it is our commitment to peace and brotherhood of all human beings living on this planet." Castro may have hoped to die with his boots on, but in the end he died only in his bedroom slippers.

Fidel Castro had held on to power longer than any other living national leader except Queen Elizabeth II. He was a huge international figure whose importance exceeded what might anyone could have expected from this little island in the sun of 11 million people. Love him … or hate him. there is probably no one else who has had as much impact on the Americas as Fidel Castro.

Castro's famous speech to the court, when he was arrested after the attack on the Moncado Barracks, closed with the statement, *"History will absolve me."* It is an open question how much absolution history will grant. Many of those who have ended up becoming become respected statemen and leaders in their own countries, have had sordid histories filled with bloodshed in order to advance their causes, ideals, and to stamp out those who opposed them. In their own countries they are memorialized as national heroes. So, what about Fidel?

What about those thousands who lost everything and fled to Miami to begin new lives . . . how much absolution will they grant? What about those who had loved ones who were executed by the Castros? Was Castro correct? Has history absolved him? Will Cuba move beyond Fidel? Interesting, and open questions.

When you go to Santiago de Cuba you will visit the Santa Ifigenia Cemetery which is the final resting place for Fidel Castro. It is here that many of the leading figures of Cuban history are buried. Fidel's tomb is oddly shaped as a seed of corn at the direction of Fidel who saw himself as planting the seed of revolution for Cuba's future. The tomb is simple with his ashes placed behind a black marble plaque that reads only "Fidel." The goose-stepping honor guard that you will see being changed around the clock, every thirty minutes, are not there primarily for Fidel, but because his tomb is located right next to the tomb of Cuba's national hero, the poet Jose Marti. The tomb of the mother of the heroic General Antonio Maceo has recently been moved to the other side of Marti's imposing grave and memorial, so the honor guard now stands watch at all three tombs.

Interestingly Fidel ordered that no roads, schools, airports or structures be named after him because he did not want a cult of personality around him or his memory. The country has respected that, but the people have adopted a living cult of memory around the phrase, "Yo soy Fidel!" "I am Fidel!" Probably a more fitting way of honoring the memory of Fidel Castro.

The movement of Fidel's ashes from Havana to Santiago de Cuba, near his birthplace, resulted in an impressive display of gratitude and respect as people lined the highways along the route grieving and honoring Fidel. Yet beneath the grief and respect one almost senses that however grateful, people are ready to turn the page.

So, what happens now?

Raul is 86 years old. Trump is 71. The Pope is 80. Heck, Sophia Loren is 83 and still hot! And Supreme Court Justice Ruth Bader Ginsberg is 84, maybe not hot but brilliant. As most of us know, there is a certain wisdom that comes with experience and age. To paraphrase Ronald Regan a bit, let us not exploit the inexperience of youth. I wouldn't write off Raul since he's very much alive! I think he understands the inter-connectiveness of the world today and I hope is pragmatic enough to encourage Cuba's progressive march forward and the relationship that has begun with the U.S. But Raul has announced his pending retirement and Cuba is ready for change.

The likely successor is Miguel Diaz-Canel, 52 years old, who trained as an electrical engineer, but has worked his way up through the Cuban Communist party for 30 years. As a young man he liked rock and roll even although it was banned as anti-revolutionary. He has served as minister of higher education, and since 2013 has been the equivalent of Raul's Vice President and has Raul's blessings to succeed him. He is firm, and some believe he will be even more authoritarian and, despite being younger, will not be receptive to the demands for change of younger Cubans. He does carry a tablet with him and wants to modernize Cuba's Internet.

Trump seems to have evoked a stronger stance from Diez-Carnel who announced after Trump's November 2017 tightening of the noose on U.S. tourism to Cuba, "We will never bow down to the imperialist aggressor." Although second in command of the military, and Cuba is a military dictatorship, unlike Raul, Diez-Carnel never appears in public in a military uniform. Raul used to say, "I am not my brother." Perhaps not wearing the uniform is Diaz-Camel's way of saying that he is not Raul.

It has been a long struggle for the Cuban people, and it still is. Amazingly they have managed to succeed. The society and government they have created is *not* our society or government, but *theirs*. Our neighbors in Cuba are by nature warm, open and friendly, and by great sacrifice have overcome enormous challenges to build t*heir* country in *their* way, reflective of their values . . . which may or may not be the same as ours.

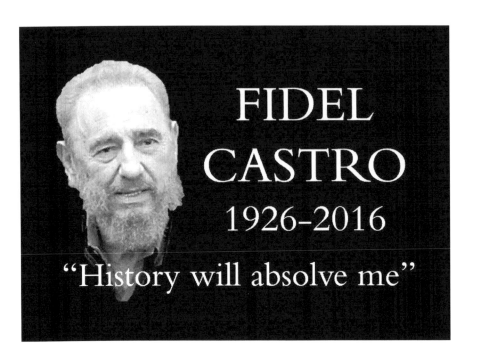

FIDEL CASTRO
1926–2016
"History will absolve me"

Fidel's tomb in Santiago de Cuba[3]

Has Cuba managed to complete its long march to a new society? Probably yes, but is it yet the fair and just and equal society that was promised? Probably not . . . just like ours. We *all have* a long way to go . . .Even in the U.S. we struggle to protect and provide *liberty . . . and justice . . . for all.*

What happens in, to, and with Cuba is not just a matter of concern for Cubans, but for *all* Americans ... North Americans, Central Americans, Caribbean Americans, and South Americans. To make America great, *ALL* of America great, we must *all* work together. Vital to that effort is how Americans in the U.S. and Americans in Cuba choose to work together as neighbors.

Cuban President Raul Castro and U.S. President Barack Obama in Panama at the Summit of The Americas 2015

The "Obama Policy" is now the "Trump Policy" with a few changes

Good Neighbors[4]

The U.S. has three neighbors: Canada with whom we share a 5,525 mile [8,891-kilometer] border with a few checkpoints, no walls; Mexico with whom we share a 1,989-mile [3,201-kilometer] border which apparently is going to be walled off, and Cuba which is just 90 miles [145 kilometers] from the southernmost point of the U.S. All three countries are our next-door neighbors.

Neighbors are funny. And how neighbors get along is funny as well. There are the neighbors from hell. Places where neighbors do not get along. And there are neighbors who are wonderful who share, and care, and get along with one another. Some neighborly relations are good, some are bad, and a little like marriages, some go through some rocky places.

We have mentioned the confused history of U.S. and Cuban relations. When Castro was still this Robin-Hood-type figure in the mountains fighting for justice, and before the Cuban Missile Crisis, Kennedy was right when he said, "To some extent it is as though Batista was the incarnation of a number of sins on the part of the United States." Well-intentioned efforts to protect the U.S. from perceived Communist threats often led to a misguided and counterproductive U.S. policy toward Cuba, driving a wedge between the two neighbors.

When Castro seized power, throwing out the U.S. approved dictator Batista and nationalizing U.S. properties in Cuba it created an even greater chasm. The Bay of Pigs Invasion followed closely by the Cuban Missile Crisis created an almost unrepairable breach in the relationship.

When the Soviet Union collapsed, and Cuba entered what it called the Special Period when people didn't have many of the necessities of life. There were shortages of food and medicine, widespread electrical outages, and civil disorder. In my opinion the U.S. missed a great opportunity just to be neighborly.

Then Cuba was struck by three hurricanes leaving 200,000 homeless, and over $5 billion U.S. in property damage. This was a golden opportunity for the U.S. to reach out and do the right thing.

Instead the U.S. persisted on a policy of isolation and embargo, punishing ordinary Cubans. And for over 50 year providing an incompetent and ineffective governmental system the opportunity to blame all its own failures on the U.S. For 50 years neighbors were pointing fingers at one another and blaming the other for all the problems.

With joint efforts by Presidents Barack Obama and Raul Castro, blessed behind the scenes by the Pope, the two leaders and their countries began engaging with one another. Enormous problems remained, questions of reparations to U.S. corporations for properties seized after the 1959 Revolution, and major problems regarding the U.S. Naval Base at Guantanamo Bay. The right for the U.S. Naval Base at Guantanamo was originally foisted upon Cuba as one of the conditions of the Platt Amendment. Cuba was forced to agree tin order to remove U.S. troops and administration, which had taken over after the Spanish Cuban American War. Further terms for Guantanamo were put in place in several follow up Treaties of Relations in which the U.S. and Cuba agreed to terms of the lease and payments. Payments Cuba claims are long past due. Cuba would like the renter out, but the renter refuses to leave or pay up.

Parenthetically, the Naval Base at Guantanamo was originally built to protect the Panama Canal. Since 2000 the Canal has been the Canal de Panama and neutral, plus the whole way of waging warfare had changed. The Guantanamo base is not only obsolete but a gigantic drain on the U.S. Treasury. But, as had been the case with the U.S. Canal Zone in Panama, there were powerful vested interests resisting any change and eager to preserve the status quo.

The Obama Executive Order permitted U.S. Americans to do what the rest of the world had been able to do all along, visit Cuba! Initially travel to Cuba was permitted mostly for family visits, and educational people to people cruises. It remains to be seen if U.S. citizens will be able to take fun and sun vacations to Cuba, just like our Canadian and European friends have been enjoying all along. Diplomatic relations were officially established, and the U.S. flag again flew at the U.S. Embassy in Havana.

So, the future looked bright for the two neighbors and for the people of both countries, and particularly for ordinary people in Cuba who had suffered and sacrificed all along, partly because of the ineptitude of their own government exacerbated by the U.S. Embargo.

But things change. As we noted, Fidel is dead, and Raul is retiring. No one is certain who will be in charge in Cuba and what their policies will be. Obama is no longer in office and Donald J. Trump is now U.S. President. During the election campaign, other than slamming his fellow Republican candidate, Florida Senator "Little" Marco Rubio, the only thing Trump said about Cuba was that "we should have gotten a better deal."

Trump ran for president criticizing everything Obama had ever done, including Obama's right to run for President even challenging Obama's birthplace. Once elected, Trump seemed intent on undoing whatever Obama had done, going down the list and checking it twice.

When he came to Obama's Executive Order permitting travel to Cuba he basically seemed only to change the title from "Obama's Executive Order on Cuba" to 'Trump's Executive Order on Cuba." Then in November 2017 he made several adjustments to his Cuba policy. Cubans, who were just getting used to welcoming U.S. Americans, held their collective breath, as did cruise and travel executives and those who had already booked cruises to Cuba.

The biggest changes, which really didn't affect cruise lines who had already been approved, was to require that U.S. Americans who wished to visit Cuba travel only on approved people to people educational trips – pretty much the same as before, but U.S. citizens would NOT BE FREE to travel independently. The Trump policy required that U.S. citizens have a sponsor or chaperone, which could be the cruise line or tour agency.

To encourage free enterprise in Cuba, which is a good thing, U.S. citizens could not patronize hotels or stores or companies that had a connection to the Cuban military – more on this in a minute! This administration, which seems bent on removing governmental regulation and bureaucracy, introduced a whole new level of regulation, bureaucracy and paperwork which had to be submitted to the U.S. Treasury Department requiring companies and individual tour and cruise passengers to maintain records of the trip for five years for possible inspection by the U.S. Treasury Department

So, that in a nutshell is why when you take a cruise to Cuba and go on an "approved" tour, which by the way is a requirement, the sponsor, or in the case of a cruise, the cruise line, must take attendance and keep records. Should your mind be spinning, don't worry! It's stupid and silly, but it won't impinge in any way on your enjoyment of your cruise. This does *not* mean that you cannot go off on your own, skip a meal onboard to eat out, or skip happy hour on board to go ashore, explore, meet some real Cubans and do your own people to people adventure, if you participate in the basic programs.

This is designed to prevent you from going off and spending a day stretched out in the sun on a lovely beach, sipping mojitos and watching beautiful bodies go by. You may live in the home of the brave and the land of the free, but, sorry pilgrim, the U.S. says you are not free to enjoy Cuba at the beach!

There are back-story elements to the new Trump polices that are very interesting and may, or may not, have anything to do with the tightened policies.

First, Cuba is not a democracy, which of course you know, but a military dictatorship. Either overtly or behind the scenes the military runs the show. In Cuba, as in some other countries, like for example Egypt, the military, in addition to being a fighting force, is also an economic and business power. That's not the way we do it in North America, but it is the way they do it in some other countries.

So, if you are, for example, a hotel builder, the way it works is that you put up the money and the Cuban government, i.e. military, gets a 54% ownership in the hotel you are building, and you as the investor get a 46% ownership. Now if the numbers work for you, fine, build your hotel. If they don't, look elsewhere. That, obviously, could bother someone who builds hotels.

This is the reason cruise lines and tour operators were given a five-page list of hotels, restaurants and stores in which the military has a part interest. According to the tightened Trump rules, these are off limits, unless of course you had the good fortune to have already signed the contract, in which case you are grandfathered in.

It is not that Trump was unfamiliar with the way things work in Cuba. According to reporting by Newsweek, "A company controlled by **Donald Trump**, the Republican nominee for president, secretly conducted business in Communist Cuba during Fidel Castro's presidency despite strict American trade bans that made such undertakings illegal, according to interviews with former Trump executives, internal company records and court filings." [5]

"Documents show that the Trump company spent a minimum of $68,000 for its 1998 foray into Cuba at a time when the corporate expenditure of even a penny in the Caribbean country was prohibited without U.S. government approval. But the company did not spend the money directly. Instead, with Trump's knowledge, executives funneled the cash for the Cuba trip through an American consulting firm called Seven Arrows Investment and Development Corp. Once the business consultants traveled to the island and incurred the expenses for the venture, Seven Arrows instructed senior officers with Trump's company—then called Trump Hotels & Casino Resorts—how to make it appear legal by linking it after the fact to a charitable effort." [6]

It is no secret that Trump is interested in a Trump branded property in Cuba. Candidate Trump told Wolf Blitzer on The Situation Room in March 2016, that he would like to open a hotel in Cuba "at the right time, when we're allowed to do it."

The Washington Post suggested, "… as the owner of a real estate company with a big stake in hotels and resorts, Trump brings an added element to an issue that is unique to his presidency — the ability, through his official actions, to undermine a growth area for his industry rivals who have raced in recent years to establish a foothold in a lucrative new market." [7]

"Starwood Hotels and Resorts, which merged with Marriott International to form the world's largest hotel chain, last year debuted the first Cuban hotel managed by a U.S. company in nearly 60 years, taking advantage of President Barack Obama's

2014 move to normalize relations with Cuba and lighten regulations enforcing the U.S. Embargo on the island."[8]

"Bloomberg reported last July that Trump Organization executives had visited Cuba on several occasions in recent years, including to visit a golf course, despite U.S. restrictions on commercial ventures."[9]

"Eric Trump, who along with his brother Donald Trump Jr, is managing the business while their father is president, told Bloomberg in a statement: 'While we are not sure whether Cuba represents an opportunity for us, it is important for us to understand the dynamics of the markets that our competitors are exploring.'" [10]

A related factor is the role of Florida Republican Senator Marco Rubio. Apparently both Rubio and Trump have laid aside their pre-adolescent, somewhat ignorant assumptions that finger size relates to genital size, and that either, or both, are somehow related to ability to govern. Trump and "Little Marco" have managed to sit down and work together, charting a future for rolling back U.S. and Cuba relations.

Rubio through the years has parlayed his Cuban heritage into becoming popular with many in the Miami Cuban exile community and being the Republican expert on Cuba. Interesting, since Rubio's parents left Cuba seeking more economic opportunities in the States, long before the Castro Revolution.

Since he ran as a serious contender for the Republican nomination as President, obviously Rubio had to have been born in the U.S., a fact never contended by Trump.

11Raul Castro for Cubans

12Father & Son

Apart from a Senatorial junket to the U.S. Naval Base at Guantanamo, although geographically on the island certainly in no way "Cuban," Marco Rubio has never actually been in the real Cuba!

I sometimes work on the ship with Victor Miret, a twenty-something Cuban American with a foot in both countries. Victor lives with his dad in Miami and his mom and sister live in Cuba where she is a university administrator. He has a great feel for the attitudes of younger Cubans in both countries. Victor has a travel agency in Miami that works primarily with business people seeking to do business in and with Cuba. He has volunteered and is eager to take Senator Rubio to visit Cuba and to show him the real Cuba, at Victor's expense.

When you return from your Cuba trip, unlike Marco Rubio, *you* will actually have seen Cuba, and met real Cuban people in Cuba thanks to your people to people adventure.

So now, it is Marco Rubio who is Trump's Republican go-to guru on Cuba, and pathway to the voting block of Florida Cuban exiles.

In many ways it is amazing that Cuba has survived and is doing so well given all the hurdles that have been placed in its path. Now the old leadership is passing on, and there is a hunger, particularly among younger people, to see their country leave the horse and wagon era and emerge into the 21st Century. There is a vacuum in Cuba and many, many needs. Some country is going to step in and give Cuba a hand. Who are the likely candidates? Russia? Cuba has been there and likely won't be that eager to enter into another Russian partnership. Will it be China? China has lots of money and is eager to invest in any way it can in Latin America. Or will it be the U.S.?

Will the U.S. continue in the spirit of neighborliness and work cooperatively and respectfully with Cuba seeking not to control or dominate but to work together to build stronger Americas?

This is not the time to roll back the clock, but a time to forge ahead for Cuba, for the United States, and for the world.

The idea of a "Good Neighbor Policy" toward Cuba is not new. Franklin D. Roosevelt began his administration with a new policy in response to growing hostility in Latin America against the U.S. for intervening in the affairs of Latin countries such as Cuba with a sense of cultural superiority. The U.S. was concerned that some Latin American countries were becoming sympathetic to Nazi Germany, and so Nelson Rockefeller was appointed to coordinate the U.S. propaganda machine to promote U.S. understanding of, and goodwill toward Latin America. This included enlisting Walt Disney himself and the Disney studios, promoting a character actress Carmen Miranda, promoting the 1939 World's Fair in New York, and even hiring Moore-McCormack Lines to take three cruise ships out of dry dock to operate a "Good Neighbor Fleet" providing cruises to Latin and South America.

Following WWII, as tensions built with the Soviet Union and the Cold War ramped up, the idea of being good neighbors was lost along the way. The dictator Batista, who had been supported and propped up by the U.S., was ousted in Cuba by Fidel and the U.S. had a Communist country on its doorstep. Fearing a "Red Tide" of Communism sweeping across Latin America, the CIA began supporting and funding other strong men and dictators who hopefully would help stop the spread of Communist ideology. The CIA began covert operations, known as "Operation Condor," to support dictatorships in Argentina, Bolivia, Brazil, Chile, Paraguay, Uruguay, Columbia, Peru, and Venezuela. The U.S. was clearly back in the business of meddling and intruding in the affairs of the families next door.

In relationships there are times when you must let go of all the garbage of the past, recommit, and start over. The same is true in relationships with neighbors. Obama actually put it very well when he said, "Neither the American, nor Cuban people are well served by a rigid policy that is rooted in events that took place before most of us were born ...   After all, these 50 years have shown that isolation has not worked. It's time for a new approach ... Today, America chooses to cut loose the shackles of the past so as to reach for a better future –- for the Cuban people, for the American people, for our entire hemisphere, and for the world."

It's time for the U.S. and Cuba to become good neighbors. If we don't, who will?

Carmen Miranda was used as a positive, if somewhat stereotypical, image of FDR's Good Neighbor Policy toward Latin America.

This "Gayest" Disney film was commissioned by the U.S. Department of State as propaganda promoting the Good Neighbor Policy

People to People

People, if you dig down beneath all the exteriors, are pretty much the same the world over. They have the same needs, fears, aspirations, but how they process all that, and how their lives develop, and the social and political impacts, are different. In that sense people *are* different. Their ideologies are different. Societies are different. Governments are different. Expectations are different. Our task as world travelers is to experience, to listen, and to learn. If you do that, you will thoroughly enjoy and love the people of Cuba, you will be enriched, and you will have a wonderful time. The Cuban people are warm, welcoming, and eager to interact with their American neighbors from the U.S.

Travel of U.S. citizens to Cuba as authorized by both the Obama and Trump Presidential Orders is for people to people educational travel. Although those of us who are U.S. citizens like to think of ourselves as a totally free people, free to travel and interact with the rest of the world, we are not free to travel to Cuba just for pleasure and rest and relaxation.

The concept of travel being about people to people is a good one, even if it is somewhat corrupted by U.S. governmental bureaucracy requiring that you, and the organization acting as your host or sponsor, maintain records that can be examined by big brother.

Travel *is* educational, even if you are just lying on the beach! But, if you want to visit Cuba, and if you are a U.S. citizen, you play along, just like Cubans often must play along with their government.

Actually, it isn't that bad! In fact, it's really a good deal since all of those "educational" excursions, which on most cruises are costly extras, are included when you go to Cuba. Yes, you will see the important tourist sites, and you will have great local guides, usually people who are well educated, educated far beyond the requirements of being a tour guide. You'll also get to visit places most typical tourists don't get to see. You'll visit artists' studios and get to chat with the artists. You'll enjoy great music and meet the local musicians. And you'll get to visit community projects and meet the people who are impacting their neighborhoods.

Plan on days that are filled with new adventures and, although you are required to participate, you are not "locked down" on a school campus or restricted on the ship. There is time when you can go off on your own, walk around town, meet people, and create your own people to people experiences. I would urge you to do so! Skip a happy hour on board and go explore the town. Forgo a meal onboard to go off and enjoy a meal in a local Paladar, one of the entrepreneurial little restaurants, frequently right in someone's home.

The Cuban people are delighted to have you as a U.S. American visiting their country. In most places the ship is docked right in town. If there is an advantage to living in a "police state" it is that you are quite safe in Cuba, particularly as a tourist. It is illegal, *very* illegal to own a firearm in Cuba.

Yes, Cubans speak Spanish. But even if you don't know Spanish, you will be able in most cases to get by and make new friends

Sharing the art form of the hat at Muralanda, a community art project in Havana

Making music with a local chamber orchestra in Cienfuegos

even if you don't have a common language. A smile, and a positive and friendly attitude is all you need. Trying to communicate without a common language can be a great deal of fun. Start with "Hola!" ["Hello!] Trust me, these folks have seen more U.S. American movies than you have seen Spanish movies! And they want to share and communicate ... with you!

My wife and I decided to forgo happy hour in Havana and go out and explore and do our own people to people adventure. We walked, and we walked, far off the beaten tourist path. In the middle of a back street in Havana we found a group of people roasting a pig in the middle of the tiny street. They were as fascinated with us as we were with them. They invited us to come back that evening and enjoy the roast pig, but. unfortunately, I had to be back on the ship.

A couple that had fled Cuba after the Castro Revolution came back home 57 years later and wanted to see the house where they had lived and which they had abandoned when they left. They got an old Yank Tank cab at the dock, drove to their old home, knocked on the door, explained who they were and were welcomed inside and shown around. In talking about their mutual lives, the lady now living there realized that a childhood friend of the former owner, our guest, still lived in the neighborhood. Together they found this other woman who had been the best friend of the lady who was our passenger when they were children. They had not seen each other for 57 years!

Another woman whose parents had survived the Holocaust knew that she had a cousin, whom she had never met, living in Havana. They got a cab and went to the Patronato Synagogue in Havana and with the help of the folks there were able to find her cousin.

We've had lots of guests skip dinner on the ship and head off to local privately owned Paladars.

Lunch at a private Paladar on the rooftop of the owner's home

Meeting with the artist who preserves both history and the memory of the old characters of Trinidad by wood carvings in the panels of old doors

The best people to people story was of a single gal on board, in her 60s, who felt sorry for the dogs she saw running around Cienfuegos. She took some cheese in a little plastic cup off the ship – generally not recommended or permitted, but anyway – and as she was leaving the port there was a guy trying to get business for his cab. This lady, who didn't speak Spanish, showed him the little cup of cheese and indicated she wanted to give it to the dogs.

The guy, who spoke only a few words of English, directed her across the street to a woman named Maria whose dog he thought had just had pups. Maria welcomed the gal from the ship, and her cheese, and showed her the dog with the pups. Without a common language they chatted, and Maria said she ought to meet her neighbor who also had a dog. So, they went to the neighbor's tiny apartment. Now all these gals are single. There is no common language other than the language of friendship.

The two Cuban gals thought that our guest really should meet yet another neighborhood gal, so the three traipsed off to another woman's tiny house. She welcomed them in and showed our guest around. She pointed out her tiny bedroom with a TV and an extra bed for when her son comes to visit. It ends up that this woman invited our guest back to visit Cuba again and warned her against wasting money on a hotel when she was welcome to stay in her home! All because of an adventurous passenger with a little cup of cheese! And no common language! So, it happens, and it can happen for you as well.

Amazing things can happen when people put aside their preconceptions, when they get governments and politics out of the way, and just share together as people.

We don't have to agree on everything or do everything the same way or think and believe the same, but we all live on the same planet, and if we're going to continue we need to cut through the crap and reach out to one another, people to people.

That's what your adventure in Cuba needs to be about.

Sugar, Rum & Slavery

Cuba has been known for producing tobacco, coffee and sugar.

When the Spanish first came to Cuba it was inhabited by the Taino people. Many of the best-know Cuban cities were originally Indigenous settlements and are still called by their Taino names, like Havana, Baracoa, Bayamo, and Camaguey. Even the name Cuba comes from the Taino language generally translated to mean "where fertile land is abundant."

When Columbus arrived in Cuba in 1492 he discovered that the Taino people were using tobacco to smoke, mostly in religious ceremonies. Tobacco was used in the Americas as far back as 1400 BC and was seen as a gift from the Creator with the ceremonial tobacco smoke carrying one's thoughts and prayers to the Creator. As Europeans returned from exploring the New World tobacco became popular in Europe with King Phillip II of Spain ordering that seeds be brought back which he planted in an area outside Toledo known for its abundance of cicadias which in Spanish are known as "cigarras."

Tobacco remains an important product in Cuba and Cuba grows what many consider to be the finest tobacco in the world. Although slaves did end up working on Cuban tobacco farms, tobacco itself didn't create the impetus for massive slavery in

Cuba. Tobacco is still a big business in Cuba and the authentic Cuban cigars are still considered the best in the world.

It takes three to four months to grow tobacco. When harvested the leaves are hung in curing barns for 45 to 60 days during which the leaves turn from green to the traditional brown color. Today tobacco is grown both outdoors and in plastic-covered greenhouses. The greenhouse tobacco has the prettiest leaves and they are used as wrapper leaves for cigars. The tobacco grown outdoors provides the other leaves that are rolled into the cigar.

Coffee growing in Cuba began mid-18th century when French farmers fleeing the revolution in Haiti began growing coffee mostly on the western plains and mountain ranges. Coffee came after the peak of importation of African slaves. In 1817 there were 191 coffee plantations. Production peaked in the 1950's and has been in decline since. Once a major Cuban export, it now makes up an insignificant portion of trade, and compared to all the other coffees worldwide, outside of local consumption there wouldn't be much demand for Cuban coffee. Before the Castro Revolution and the nationalization of the coffee industry Cuba was producing 60,000 tons of coffee a year, today something like 6,000 tons.

To stretch the coffee supply, Cubans use a blend of coffee and ground roasted chickpeas. It's warm, brown, rustic, high in caffeine, and most people add sugar to make it drinkable. Because of the limited quantity of coffee, the drink is always consumed in small amounts from small cups known as "tacitas."

At the turn of the 20th century, Havana had more than 150 cafes. There are small local cafes with aging equipment as well as fancier, newer cafes mostly for tourists. But most people can't afford that luxury, so they get their coffee from a "ventanilla," a small window in someone's home from which an entrepreneurial Cuban is selling coffee. A tiny cup from a ventanilla costs a couple of Cuban pesos, of Cuban peso, the equivalent of about 10 cents U.S. Cheap, but if you're only taking home *$20 a month* . . . So just like at Starbucks. in the morning people line up outside the ventanillas, and like most things in Cuba, Cubans with limited resources make it work.

The crop that had overwhelming economic, cultural and social impact, and was most connected to the slave trade, was sugar.

Europeans didn't know sugar until the Arabs and Berbers introduced sugar to Western Europe when they conquered the Iberian Peninsula in the 8th Century. The Crusaders also brought sugar home with them after their campaigns in the Holy Land, where they encountered caravans carrying "sweet salt". The Crusade chronicler William of Tyre described sugar as "very necessary for the use and health of mankind."

Europeans quickly developed a sweet tooth. The only problem was that Sugarcane cultivation requires a tropical or subtropical climate, with a minimum of 24 inches of annual moisture and about the only places in Europe where sugar could be grown was in southernmost Spain and on the Canary Islands. Because of its scarcity, across Europe sugar became the ultimate luxury. Royals exchanged gifts of grand gold, silver, and china sugar cellars and the sugar inside was more valuable than the container.

Sugar got to the Americas because a 41-year-old adventurer stopped in the Canary Islands to re-provision his ships with wine and water before setting out across the sea. He intended to stay only four days but had the good fortune to meet a local woman over drinks one evening and a passionate romance ensued. The woman turned out to be the Governor of the island, Beatrice de Bobadilla, and he stayed a month. When he left, she gave her lover cuttings of sweet sugar cane with which he could remember his sweetheart back in the Canary Islands.

His name was Christopher Columbus and on his second voyage to the "new world," Columbus brought sugar cane cuttings, first to Hispaniola, later to become Haiti and the Dominican Republic, and then on to Cuba. Sugar cultivation would become very important in for all three areas, and the growth of the sugar industry in Haiti would have serious impact on Cuba.

In the Americas the Spanish found the ideal conditions for growing sugar. The West Indies may not have been as full of gold as the Spaniards had hoped, but the islands could still provide a valuable service to the Spanish Empire by providing sugar. Sugar wasn't just about growing the cane: it was an entire industry. After the cane was harvested it had to be quickly washed, then pressed by giant mills and the juice collected, treated, filtered and boiled to a dark syrup that either could be dried as crystalized sugar, or boiled down and distilled to produce rum.

Growing sugar was tiring, hot, dangerous work that required large number of workers, intensely coordinated and controlled. Workers in the cane fields cut the sugar by hand with the sun boiling down, temperatures 98 degrees Fahrenheit with 99% humidity. And these fields were filled with rats and snakes – lots of snakes. This wasn't exactly the kind of work that appealed to the European settlers, so the earliest plantations used Indigenous natives as indentured slaves.

The Tainos were the first Indigenous people the Europeans met. Columbus, believing he was in the outer islands of India, called this new world the "West Indies" and he called these Indigenous people "Indians."

When sugar first came to Cuba, the Tainos became the indentured slaves of the Spanish settlers to work in the sugar industry. The Tainos didn't understand why they had to clear fields, mostly in the central plains between Havana, Trinidad and East towards Santiago to grow cane for their new masters while doing without their original crops and food

When Europeans came to Cuba they discovered the Taino people using and smoking tobacco.

[13]Cuba and the Cuban sugar industry was built on the backs of African slaves.

source. Eventually, without their traditional food supply, combined with the introduction of European diseases for which they had no immunity, the Taino died off, leaving the Spanish sugar growers without the labor they required.

So, they began to import slave labor from Africa. For the next three and a half centuries, slaves of African origin provided most of the labor for the sugar industry. It has been said that the entire New World enterprise depended on the enormous and expandable flow of slave labor from Africa.

The sugar plantations began to depend on slave labor which was either imported and purchased legally or smuggled into Cuba. The lack of labor and the difficulty of importing slaves limited the growth of the sugar industry.

The biggest change in the sugar industry, and for Cuba as a whole, came when the British Invaded Havana in 1762 and occupied the island. They eliminated the Spanish trade restrictions and suddenly sugar farms had access to equipment and goods from Europe and America. They were able to import slaves without restrictions, and the British were the leading slave traders in the world. Although the British only occupied Cuba for 11 months, the changes were dramatic. The British period ended when the Seven Years War in Europe came to an end and in the Treaty of Paris England traded Cuba back to Spain in exchange for Florida.

Sugar became one of the first luxuries consumed by the masses in Western societies followed by coffee, tobacco and chocolate ... and the demand was great. When the British introduced and expanded trade with Europe and North America, the sugar industry boomed in Cuba. Sugar production increased almost overnight. Sugar exports prior to the English occupation had averaged 300 tons a year, then within a year after the invasion production and exports grew dramatically. From 1763 to 1769 sugar production averaged 2,000 tons a year. By 1774 there were more than 44,000 African slaves in Cuba.

Sugar and the byproduct rum introduced globalization to the world. The Triangle Trade was an efficient, if inhuman, way to use ships and keep them producing revenue through a worldwide system of commerce. From the late 16th to early 19th century ships would take sugar and molasses from the Caribbean to New England. Barrels of rum would then be loaded onto the ships to Europe where the rum was traded for European goods that were traded and used to purchase slaves in Africa. The slaves where then taken to the Caribbean and sold and the whole cycle started over again.

Places like Newport, Rhode Island and Boston, Massachusetts made some of the best rum in the world. To give you an idea, when the U.S.S CONSTITUTION, "Old Ironsides", sailed from Boston in 1798 with 475 crew and officers she loaded 48,600 gallons of fresh water and 79,400 gallons of rum! That was a record for a ship taking on rum for a voyage held until modern day cruise ships came along.

Sugar became king in Cuba. By 1790 sugar production had soared and the number of slaves had doubled. It was the major industry and source of revenue. Then in 1791 there was a slave rebellion on Hispaniola in the French colony of San Dominique, later to become Haiti, which at the time was the largest producer of sugar in the world.

During the Haitian slave revolt more than 180 sugar plantations and 900 coffee plantations were destroyed. More than 2,000 Europeans and 10,000 African slaves lost their lives. Sugar production and exports plummeted on Hispaniola and many of the French planters fled to Cuba bringing their expertise to the areas around Cienfuegos east to Santiago de Cuba.

As demand increased and steam technology made production more efficient, plantations grew in size and complexity. Sugar mills began buying up neighboring plantations to insure a steady supply of raw material. The sugar production and wealth exploded after 1830 when railroads were imported into Cuba from the U.S. This technology made the sugar industry more and more dependent on U.S. engineering and companies.

A traditional way of raising sugar cane involved burning the cane field before harvesting it to rid the field of rats and snakes and making the cane stalks easier to harvest. Because this area around Cienfuegos was a major producer of sugar cane, calling this the land of "a hundred fires" might have made sense. But it was nothing so exciting. Cienfuegos has the rather uninteresting history of being named after Jose Cienfuegos, Captain General of Cuba in the early 1800s.

As their wealth increased the owners of the sugar mills began building lavish mansions like those in Trinidad and Cienfuegos. The sugar industry provided great wealth at least for a few people. One of the examples of this great wealth is the Moorish-looking Palacio de Valle on the edge of Cienfuegos Harbor that was built as the private house of the wealthiest sugar merchant in Cuba. Today it houses a restaurant, but the terrace is open to the public. The façade has three towers of different design symbolizing power, religion, and love.

Palacio Ferrer on the main square in Cienfuegos was built as the summer home of another sugar merchant. The famous Italian tenor Enrico Caruso stayed here when he performed up the street. The theater where he sang is named Teatro Tomas Terry built by another sugar merchant who became wealthy through the slave trade. In his last will and testament, he left money to build the theater where Enrico Caruso and Sarah Bernhardt performed.

Trinidad also benefited from the wealth of the sugar industry. The Palacio Cantero, built in 1828 by a planter whose fortune was ill-gotten, is as beautiful as its owner was unscrupulous. Today it is the Museo Municipal de Historia with an eclectic collection of furnishings and artifacts.

[14]Palacio de Valle on the edge of Cienfuegos Harbor built by one of the wealthiest sugar merchants in Cuba.

Another sugar merchant summer home, Palacio Ferrer on the central Plaza Marti in Cienfuegos.

At the bottom of the square is the House of Mayor Ortiz, built in 1809 by Ortiz de Zúníga, who later became Mayor of Trinidad. The house shows many of the typical features of Trinidadian houses, including the large entrance door with two smaller doors cut into it, the "barrotes," what we might think of as bars. These are a feature of Latin architecture even to this day and the reason is that these folks didn't have air conditioning. The air conditioning was open windows. If you want your windows open all night, you'd better have something to keep the dogs and thieves out. The projecting balcony is another feature of Spanish colonial architecture. The family typically lived on the second floor and the balcony made it possible not only to enjoy the breezes but to watch what was going on in the square. Today it is an art museum of mostly contemporary art with a great view of the square from the balcony.

The biggest impact came from all the West African people who were imported, not as people, but as merchandise to be sold, traded, used, abused and who were basically just possessions who literally were worked to death, then replaced by other slaves.

About the time Cuba's sugar industry was booming, slaves became more and more expensive to buy. There was even talk around the Caribbean of emptying out the prisons of Europe and bringing white convicts over as indentured slaves to provide a labor force, which is basically what the French did in French Guiana and the famed Devil's Island. Additionally, you had the slave uprising in Haiti with other uprisings following. The idea was taking hold that these were indeed people who should be treated humanely and ... *be free*. All of that impacted the sugar production industry.

Trinidad's distinctive birdcage *barrotes*, allowed for windows to be left open overnight to allow maximum air circulation.

Decaying old Cuban sugar train near the dock in Cienfuegos.

The English had abolished slave *trading* in 1807 although they didn't abolish slavery until 1833. But because the English had been the largest slave traders, after abolishing slave trading they actively tried to stop the trade. This made life difficult for the sugar industry. Never-the-less Cuba illegally imported some 400,000 slaves after 1820, most working on plantations producing sugar, molasses and rum.

In Matanzas, Cuba in 1844 there was a slave rebellion that resulted in 4,000 arrests including freed slaves, mulattoes and Creoles. That uprising was led by, a slave named Carlota. Seventy-eight of the rebellious slaves were shot and more than a hundred were whipped to death. The special treatment given Carlota was that while alive she was tied to two horses that we sent to run in opposite directions in order to rip her body apart. Slavery was gradually phased out between 1879 and 1886, during which time the U.S. Civil War erupted.

At the beginning of the U.S. Civil war some of the sugar people saw the Southern States as possibly allies, but that didn't work out too well. So, you had slavery officially outlawed, the U.S. freeing the slaves, the South losing the Civil War in the U.S., and Spain cracking down on Cuban dissent. But the sweet air of freedom was in the air, not just for slaves, but also for tiny Cuba anxious to be free from Spain. It would take three decades before the Spanish-Cuban-American War finally ended slavery in Cuba.

Throughout this period life was getting more and more difficult for the sugar industry. The large sugar estates that remained faced an uncertain future. Slavery was gone. They needed money to invest in modernizing their facilities if they were to survive. Interest rates were high, and in 1880 a law was passed that allowed creditors to seize the land of those in default. In 1884 it was reported that "out of the 12 or 13 hundred planters on the island, not a dozen is thought to be solvent." Cuba had no choice but to turn to the U.S. for a market in sugar and for capital. U.S. investors quickly landed the deal lending money with high interest rates, then foreclosing, and buying industries for pennies on the dollar. This would set the stage for the enormous U.S. investment in Cuba, which of course was brought to a screeching halt in 1959 by the Revolution and the nationalization of all those U.S. investments. Because of the U.S. blockade the remaining factories have been unable to get replacement parts, with the result being that only a few, antiquated processing plants remain in operation.

Much of the culture, heritage, and tradition of Cuba today goes back to that enormous influx of slave labor from Western Africa that fueled, but never shared in, the success of the Cuban sugar industry. There are records of those slaves who were brought in legally, but only guestimates to the numbers of those who were brought in illegally. No nobody knows for sure how many were forcibly ripped from their homes in West Africa and brought to the strange world of Cuba to live and die. Of those who left Africa many would die or get sick in route, and dead or alive, they were viewed as damaged goods and thrown overboard at sea. It is estimated about one tenth of all the slaves brought to the New World were brought to Cuba which had enormous impact on the history of Cuba and its culture.

These people struggled to keep the traditions of their African homelands alive, so the music, the dancing, the rhythm all were expressions of yearnings and beliefs that could not be openly expressed. Much of this was forbidden and repressed because slave owners were threatened and knew they were in many cases outnumbered. It is from Africa that much of the Cuban tradition of dance, festival and celebration originate, and much of the spiritual traditions of Cuba originates.

Cuba was once the world's largest sugar exporter. Until the 1960s, the U.S. received 33% of its sugarcane imports from Cuba. During the cold war, Cuba's sugar exports were bought with subsidies from the Soviet Union. After the collapse of this trade arrangement, coinciding with a collapse in sugar prices, two thirds of sugar mills in Cuba closed, and 100 000 workers lost their jobs. Some sugar is still exported to China and a lot is for domestic consumption. If the rapprochement with the U.S. continues I am sure there are hopes for a rebound not only exporting sugar, but also exporting genuine Cuban rum.

The most famous producer of Cuban rum was Bacardi which began in 1862. Facundo de Bacardi y Moreau bought a small distillery in Santiago de Cuba and using Cuban molasses began making a rum that was lighter than the heavier rum produced by most Caribbean islands and being made in New England. Bacardi built its market position in the U.S. during Prohibition, edging out the old New England rum. Shiploads of Bacardi went to rendezvous with the rum-runners just outside American territorial waters. After the 1959 Revolution Bacardi fled from Cuba to Puerto Rico and Miami. The way spirits companies and brands bounce around, today Bacardi is owned by a giant French company.

The beautiful art deco Bacardi headquarters building can be seen in Havana with its name still clearly emblazoned over the entrance.

In 1878 another Cuban began producing Havana Club rum. Today the rum still being produced in the old Bacardi distillery in Santiago de Cuba is called simply Santiago. Both are widely available in Cuba.

Today the sugar cane is harvested by giant machines taken in and crushed. The juice is boiled down to molasses, mixed with water and fermented. It is then distilled either in pot stills or in a column still, usually the light rums in the column still and the darker rums in the traditional pot still. Rum, and especially the rich dark rums, is a spirit that improves with age and it ages best in 40-gallon oak barrels that have been charred on the inside. The permeability of the oak allows air to pass through, and this mellows the rum. The oak also gives the rum its warm, golden color.

Bacardi Building in Havana.

Emilio Bacardi's tomb in Santa Ifigenia Cemetery in Santiago de Cuba.

Faith & Religion in Cuba

The two main religions in Cuba are the Roman Catholic version of Christianity and Afro-Cuban Santeria. Of course, there are other religions as well. If you walk around Havana, you will pass by the Abdallah Mosque in Old Havana. There are three active synagogues in Havana, as well as Jehovah's Witnesses, Bahai and other groups. There are Baptist, Methodist and Pentecostal churches. So religious faith is alive and well in Cuba.

We were in Havana one Sunday morning and I walked into the Catedral de San Cristobal during mass and was surprised to find that not only was the church packed, but many of the people, maybe most of them, were younger people. Probably far more young folks than you might find in many churches in the U.S.

There are many layers of religious faith and superstition in Cuba, and just when you think you've encountered them all, you discover yet another layer. Things in Cuba are not always what they appear to be at first glance, and that is true of faith and religion as well.

Most educational trips to Cuba are going to include a visit to El Cobre, the most important shrine for Cubans and most famous church in the country. It is located outside of Santiago de Cuba in the foothills of the Sierra Maestra near the old copper mines that give it its commonly used name, "El Cobre," meaning literally in Spanish "The Copper." But the official name of the triple-domed church is a mouthful, "The Church of Our Lady of Charity of Copper."

The legend of Our Lady of Charity, sometimes just referred to as "El Cobre," is that the original image was brought by Spanish colonists who came around 1606 from Toledo, Spain where a similar image of the Virgin Mary of Charity was already being venerated. The image was carried by Spanish seafarers to protect them from pirates. The story goes that two Indigenous brothers, Rodrigo and Juan de Hoyos, and an African slave child named Juan Moreno, henceforth known as the "three Juans," set out in a small boat to get salt for the preservation of meat. While out in the bay a storm came up, violently tossing about their small boat. Juan, the slave boy, was wearing a medal with the image of the Virgin Mary so the three began to pray for her protection. Suddenly, the skies cleared, and the storm was gone. In the distance, they saw a strange object floating in the water. They rowed towards it as the waves brought it towards them. At first, they mistook it for a bird, but quickly saw that it was what seemed to be a statue of a girl. At last they were able to determine that it was a statue of the Virgin Mary holding the child Jesus on her left arm and holding a gold cross in her right hand. The statue was fastened to a board with an inscription saying "Yo Soy la Virgen de la Caridad" or "I am the Virgin of Charity." Much to their surprise, the statue had remained completely dry while afloat in the water.

With the wooden statue in their grasp, the three Juans miraculously made it to shore. The dark-skinned Virgin Mary of Charity statue has become "The Queen of the Cubans" and pilgrims come to the El Cobre, often on their knees, to pray to the image and place mementos and offerings of thanksgiving for her miracles. Among those are small boats and prayers for those who tried to make it to Florida on rafts. The image is revered as the protectoress of Cuba and has been visited by, among others, Pope John Paul II who blessed the statue in 1998.

The image of the Virgin is dressed in yellow, wears a crown of emeralds, diamonds, and rubies, and encased in glass high above the altar. The actual statue has only been removed from the church three times, but copies of the statue are paraded in the streets on special festival days.

Capilla de los Milagros or the "Chapel of Miracles" is a small room that holds a wide variety of offerings to Our Lady of Charity, from the humblest of offerings to precious jewels to votive offerings of gold and precious stones. There are sports trophies, military decorations, African dirt brought back by Cuban soldiers, even clippings from the beards of some of the Cuban rebels who fought with Castro in the Sierra Maestra Mountains. There is even the Nobel Prize medal for Literature awarded to Ernest Hemingway, who personally placed it at the feet of the Patron Saint of Cuba.

Fidel Castro, as mentioned, was the son of Angel Castro, a self-made sugar farmer from Spain. His family was moderately wealthy and sent young Fidel to Catholic elementary school, and to a prep school run by Jesuit priests. So, Fidel had a religious background, but after the revolution in 1959 he declared Cuba to be an atheist state, closed Catholic educational institutions and churches and sent priests to work camps calling them out as "symbols of great wealth."

The collapse of the Soviet Union and its support for Cuba, either forced or gave Cuba the opportunity to develop its own form of socialism. In 1991 the Communist Party began to allow believers into its ranks and in 1992, the constitution was amended to remove the definition of Cuba as being a state based on Marxism–Leninism, and Article 42 was added, which prohibited discrimination based on religious belief. Restrictions began to be lessened and the Popes started making calls on an aging and ailing Fidel. Cuba is no longer an atheist state, but, like many other countries, is a secular state, just like the U.S. Like the U.S., it also has a rich Christian heritage, some of it good, and some of it, like slavery in both countries, evil and contrary to Christianity.

Even during the "atheist" years, religious faith and practice, although often quiet and underground, remained an important part of Cuban society and life.

When the Spanish arrived, they came with the authority of the Crown and the church, ostensibly not just to increase the power of Spain, but also to promote the Christian faith, even if it meant doing so at the point of a sword.

As noted, originally the island was inhabited by Taino Arawak people. In October 1492 Columbus arrived and claimed the island for Spain. The first Spanish settlement was at Baracoa in 1511, and Havana was settled in 1515. The Indigenous people who were here when Columbus came were virtually wiped out, not just by the harshness and oppression of the Spanish settlers, but by diseases for which the locals had no immunity.

Cuba developed slowly but importantly as an urbanized society that primarily supported the Spanish colonial empire. Cuba was a major rendezvous point for Spanish Treasure Fleet. During the Seven Years' War British captured Cuba, but Britain ruled only one year until Peace of Paris gave Britain Florida in exchange for Cuba. But in that one year of British rule, Cuba changed dramatically. Trade was introduced between Cuba and North America and other islands in the Caribbean. Most importantly, the British developed the sugar industry, which would dominate much of Cuban life, and began importing slaves.

Africans were ripped from their homelands and herded onto the slave ships to be taken to strange lands like Cuba where they were sold and branded like cattle. All they had left was the memories and cultural beliefs and religion of their homeland, forbidden, but kept hidden deep within their souls.

The music, the dancing, the rhythm all were expressions of yearnings and beliefs that could not be openly expressed. All of this entered the history and the religious life of Cuba and it is from Africa that much of the Cuban tradition of dance, festival

Cathedral of Saint Christopher, Havana

African slaves brought with them traditions of music, dance and religion.

and celebration originate, and much of the spiritual traditions of Cuba as well. The strongest mix of Spanish and African culture is seen In and around Santiago de Cuba, reflected in art and architecture, music and dance, and in the local cuisine. The weather in Santiago is the hottest in Cuba, and many of those African traditions became the basis for the hottest celebration in Cuba, Carnival in Santiago! Carnival in Cuba is not related to Lent but traditionally was a time of celebration, introduced by slaves, that was held after the harvest was over.

The Roman Catholic Church in Cuba, as in much of Latin America, is the same as the church in Rome, but it expresses itself in different ways, and it has been influenced by local cultures and unofficially incorporated aspects of traditional African religion. And the African religions, as a matter of survival, incorporated great swaths of traditional Catholicism. This concept of accommodation is nothing new. Theologians have always believed that God, who is a spirit, unknowable and unreachable by definition, has through the person of Jesus communicated himself to humanity in a way to which humans can respond, and in that way come to know God.

Early Christians fearing persecution, accommodated themselves to the Roman Saturnalia tradition, conveniently setting the celebration of the birth of Christ to coincide with the Roman Saturnalia celebration, knowing that the Romans would be too wasted to give them hassle. Where it is most effective today, the church has accommodated its traditions to local custom. We don't expect Indigenous people to wear suits and ties, dresses, hats and gloves to worship God. We don't necessarily expect young people to appreciate the music of Bach and Handel in church, so we accommodate the service to more contemporary musical tastes. In cultures where there is widespread religious superstition, the church has embraced superstition as a cultural aspect, which is the case with the veneration of the El Cobre statue.

What you have today in Cuba is the strange melding of aspects of traditional Christianity with traditional African spiritualism. On the surface it would appear that Cuba is predominantly Christian and mostly Catholic, with maybe 70% claiming some Christian identity, but perhaps more significant are the 30% who identify themselves as nonreligious, really about the same as in the U.S.

Pope Francis, when he was Archbishop of Buenos Aires wrote that the Revolutionary government in Cuba, "seeking to diminish the Church's presence in the island and in a bid to dismantle its pastoral work, has fostered and allowed the growth and expansion of other cults—such as Santeria—in an effort to provide a bit of spiritual relief to Cubans," The melding of Christianity with beliefs rooted in African religion has long been a fact of life in Cuba, if at times an uncomfortable one for the Catholic Church, which frowns on the mixing of faiths.

With the traditional African spiritualism and cults like Santeria, there wasn't, and still isn't, any official accommodation, but people just tended to blend things together. Take El Cobre and the Virgin of Charity. On the surface it is Catholicism, but for many nominal Catholics in Cuba, devotion to the Virgin of Charity is associated with the Afro-Cuban cult of Oshun the goddess of rivers, gentleness, femininity and love who is also always depicted as a beautiful black woman dressed in yellow. In Santeria the Virgin of El Cobre, and the more sensuous image of the beautiful African goddess Oshun, are combined in prayers and home altars. And something similar happens with the Virgin of Mercy and Obatala.

The Yoruba people, who came from Africa, what is today Nigeria, brought customs of trance and divination, a system for communicating with ancestors, along with animal sacrifice, sacred drumming and dance. Beginning around 1515 they accommodated their traditions to the Catholic tradition of saints. This was a convenient a way to hide in plain sight their forbidden traditional beliefs in a hostile culture dominated by slavery. In that surreptitious way they could practice their religion while appearing to be celebrating the religion of their masters. By syncretizing their native religion with the religion of their masters they could hide in plain sight.

The main god of Santeria is Olofi, who is similar to the God of Christianity and Judaism, but without contact with the Earth. The lesser gods mediate between Olofi and the faithful on Earth. These lesser gods, like saints, are called orishas and listen to the prayers of believers, with each having certain specialties. Followers look to one or more orishas to protect them and guide them throughout life. There are around 400 orishas. It sounds like a lot but is nowhere near the 3,300 Hindu gods. Only eight of the orishas are regularly worshiped in Cuba, and the ones most revered are Obatala, Oshun, Vemaya, and Chango.

Unlike Christianity, Santeria does not have an edifice complex, so instead of grand churches and temples, the practice of Santeria centers around home altars and local shrines. Santeria involves many ceremonies, some of which may be conducted in homes, others in the outdoors. In recent years in Cuban Santeria has worked to be thought of as a religion rather than an African cult.

In Cuba you will often see men and women dressed all in white. This is not just a fashion statement or a recognition that white is a good color to wear in a hot and humid climate. People who are striving to become Santeros, or a kind of Santeria priest, wear white for a year and abstain from various activities as a symbol of purity. White is the color of Obatala, the most important orisha not only because he is the protector of the head, but because he is the main intermediary between Olofi and humans. It's not sexist to call Obatala a he or she since Obatala is a hermaphrodite.

Obatala's followers flock daily to the La Merced Catholic Church in the oldest part of Havana to venerate the Virgin of Mercy who, has an important role in their belief quite apart from the role of the Virgin Mary in Catholicism.

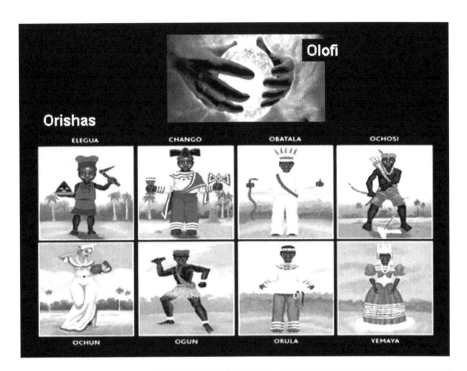

Obatala, is a hermaphrodite god, protector of the head as well as the main intermediary between Olofi and humans

Oshun, is the goddess of love, lives in rivers, and corresponds to the Virgen of Cobre

Vemaya, is the sea goddess & mother of orishas, wears blue, capable of great sweetness & great anger, linked with the Virgin de Regala in Havana who is the Christian saint of fishermen

Chango, is the virile & sensual god of fire & war who adores dancing, and corresponds to Saint Barbara

Vemaya, is the sea goddess and mother of orishas ... all these others ... wears blue, is capable of great sweetness and great anger just like the ocean. She is linked with the Virgin de Regala in Havana who is the Christian protector of fishermen.

Chango, whose color is red, is the virile and sensual god of fire and war who adores dancing and corresponds to St Barbara.

Oshun, whose color is yellow, is the goddess of love, lives in rivers, and corresponds to the Virgen del Cobre.

The movie "Strawberry and Chocolate" has both a cute and sad story line set against a very difficult time in Cuba when intellectuals, artists, religious, gay, and anyone who thought differently than the Revolution was considering leaving and escaping. It's a good movie, one which anyone interested in Cuba should watch. If you knew nothing about Santeria you would miss much of the subtext of the movie which illustrates how the hopes, dreams and choices of daily living are connected to faith in Oshun.

For many Cubans who are both Roman Catholic and followers of Santeria, a visit to El Cobre is like a two-for-one. You can kill two birds with one stone, and not incidentally people used to take little copper stones that came from the old copper mines in El Cobre as a talisman of Oshun and the Virgin of Charity. So, when you make your request or offering to the Virgin of Charity at the same time you are taking care of Oshun.

Pretty much everything in Cuba has this subtext of Santeria. You choose to paint your house blue because your orisha is Vemaya. You wear yellow because of your devotion to Oshun. You choose white because you seek the protection of Obalata.

Things are not always what they seem to be on the surface in Cuba. For example, there is a picture that is frequently used in travel-related materials about Cuba. Unfortunately for me, it is copyrighted and expensive to use. It shows two women, dressed mostly in white, smoking cigars. To understand that picture you must look below the surface. Yes, they may just enjoy cigars, but in Santeria smoking a cigar can be part of religious practice, since the cigar smoke is viewed to have a cleansing effect, much like holy water in the Roman Catholic tradition. The colors of the red and yellow flowers in their hair, the white dresses, the blue sweater the one gal is wearing, the color of the beads they are wearing, none of this is by chance. Everything has deeper, spiritual, and religious significance.

Ceremonies are an important part of Santeria. They may be private, held in a home, or more complicated productions performed outdoors.

Healing ceremonies make use of natural elements and herbs and are an important aspect of Santeria belief.

For those who live by this religion, animal sacrifice is not just about killing the animals for the sake of participating in an unconventional ritual. This may seem unconventional, at least to those who do not have an Abrahamic religious background, i.e. are not Jewish, Christian or Muslim, since all these Abrahamic religions have important backgrounds of animal sacrifice. A key aspect for all religions who use sacrifice is that "the life is in the blood."

Sacrifice is a key concept for the traditional Jewish and Islamic sacrificial systems. The reason why Christians practice communion is to celebrate the sacrifice of Christ on the cross. The Roman Catholic Church believes that at the moment of the Mass the wine and bread actually and really become the body and blood of Christ.

In Santeria, the sacrifice is an offering to the orishas performed for major ceremonies. The blood is for the orishas, and the meat is for the Santeros, and after the ritual, the animal is eaten. That may sound a little different to folks whose protein usually comes shrink-wrapped in plastic from the local super market chain, or

A Santeria priest explains his beliefs to a tour group in small community worship altar dedicated to Vemaya.

[15]A Santeria ceremony conducted in home.

in a bucket from KFC. I know some people hear about religious animal sacrifice and say, "But what about the poor animal?" Meanwhile they are chowing down a Big Mac at McDonald's. It's all in what you are used to.

Is Santeria the same as voodoo? It is, and it isn't . . . Both have a supreme being served by spirits, either the "orishas" of Santeria, or the "loas" or "laws" of voodoo. Both have hierarchy of spirits identified with Catholic saints. Both brought by slaves from Nigeria but from different tribes and influenced by the cultures where they were enslaved. Those who developed Santeria came from areas influenced by Spanish Catholicism. Those who developed Voodoo came mostly from French influenced areas. Santeria is the primary spiritual belief system for much of Cuba and Voodoo is the primary spiritual belief system and the official religion of Haiti.

As if all that weren't complicated enough, there is more ... other layers if you will, of Cuban faith and religion.

It is estimated that something like 430,000 slaves were brought to North America, whereas over 700,000 African slaves were brought to the island of Cuba. In the United States, much of the slave population grew by natural increase, that is slaves who were born in the U.S.A. Life for slaves on Cuban sugar plantations was so harsh that slaves were literally worked to death, requiring more slaves to be brought from Africa. Fewer women were purchased to work in Cuba so there were fewer children. Cuban slaves came from a broader geographical swath of Africa and even in one general area of Africa there were variations in religious tradition. Because Cuba burned through the lives of many slaves so rapidly, and because slavery lasted so long in Cuba, many of the slaves had more recently been brought from Africa and had fresher memories of their traditional faith systems.

Those who came from the Yorba region brought with them the African religious tradition that became Santeria. Those from the

Congo area brought with them yet another religious tradition, a more secretive tradition known as Palo, and presenting yet another layer of religious life in Cuba. The practitioners of Palo are secretive, so nobody knows for sure how many followers there are in Cuba.

Palo deals in life spirits and powers, magical powers if you will, powers that can be used for good or evil. They believe that all natural objects, particularly sticks, are infused with powers linked to the spirits and spiritual powers. A follower of Palo may have a pot-looking receptacle of sticks sitting in the corner that to many North Americans would look like kindling for the fireplace. But in Palo these sticks represent serious powers. This is not Harry Potter gone wild, but a serious belief system intended to control the forces of nature. A person either has or is given when initiated, a nganga, which is a strong spiritual energy of a dead person's spirit. In the past that nganga was prepared by raiding a recent tomb and burying a part of a deceased person under the dirt floor of one's hut. In the practice today herbs, music, drums, herbs are widely, chalk drawings, and symbols, Beads, shells, and animal sacrifices are used to contact the spirits and see into the future. Symbols are sometimes tattooed onto one's body to indicate life forces and spirits. There are two groups within Palo, one that incorporates the crucifix and Roman Catholic saints, and the other which does not.

Things are not always what they appear to be in Cuba, nor are they simple. Various levels of religious faith and superstition merge together in strange and interesting ways. And all of this has managed to survive and outlive the Marxist-Leninist ideal of the atheist state.

I ask a young Cuban friend to explain his religious beliefs and he tells me, "It's complicated" and he would probably cringe at my attempts to explain.

It is complicated. He is a baptized Roman Catholic and wears a rosary that he was careful to have blessed. He also wears a red bead choker around his neck, not just because it looks cool, but because the color represents one of his protective orishas. He wears a really cool beaded bracelet and when I asked where I could get one, he answered, "You can't." It is the symbol of his advancing in the Santeria religion to the point where he is Santero or Santeria priest.

I've never seen him without his shirt, but I can see part of a tattoo on his chest that looks like a Palo drawing of his life force. I know he has an Arabic tattoo inside his arm which I'm sure relates to Islamic influence in Africa on the segments of the Yoruba religion, since there was a Muslim influence in parts of Africa when slaves were being shipped off to Cuba.

He's a sensitive, serious guy, and obviously covering all the bases of Cuban faith and religion. He has developed his own synergistic religion and he sees no conflict in his system. He patiently explains to me that Olofi, the main god of Santeria, is the same as the Lord God that I and the Catholic Church worship. He points out that we both love and worship the same Jesus Christ. He's a good guy, searching and trying to do the right things, and although he has a different background and different take on life, since we have the same Father, I consider him a brother.

Candidate Donald Trump stuck his foot in it when he was fighting Ted Cruz for the nomination. Ted Cruz' father is an evangelical, Cuban-immigrant pastor. After trying to implicate Cruz' father in the assassination of Kennedy, Trump questioned if indeed there really were any evangelicals in Cuba.

Actually, the evangelical Christian church, traditional denominations and Pentecostal denominations, compose one of the fastest growing religious groups in Cuba. So, although still a minority, the evangelical[16] protestant church in Cuba is alive and growing. One of the differences of the evangelical church is that

In viewing every Christian as a "saint," as in "when the saints go marching in," it doesn't have the tradition or superstition of venerating saints and objects. With a faith grounded in the belief that God's Holy Spirit lives in his followers, one does not have to worry about seeking the protection of saints, or orishas, since "the one who is in you is greater than the one who is in the world." (1 John 4:4)

Hemingway & Cuba

Ernest Miller Hemingway was born on July 21, 1899, in the Chicago suburb of Oak Park, Illinois. His father was a doctor and his mother was a musician. Both were well-educated and respected members of the Oak Park community. Another Oak Park resident, architect Frank Lloyd Wright, would describe it as "so many churches for so many good people to go to." The family lived in a sprawling seven-bedroom home. His mother insisted on Ernest taking cello lessons and later he would admit that although he hated the lessons, they were useful in his writing. Hemingway attended Oak Park and Forest High School where he took part in boxing, football, water, and track and field. He excelled in English classes and wrote for the school newspaper.

His family liked to spend summers in Upper Michigan near Petoskey where his father taught Hemingway to hunt, fish, and camp creating a passion for outdoor adventure.

After high school, Hemingway became a cub reporter for The Kansas City Star but the job only lasted six months. That brief stint instilled in Hemingway the way of writing outlined in the newspaper's style guide: short sentences, short first paragraphs, vigorous English, and a positive approach. He churned out articles for the paper with compelling titles like "Laundry Car

Over Cliff," "The Fighting Flea" and "At The End of the Ambulance Run."

Early in 1918, at the age of nineteen, Hemingway signed on to become an ambulance driver for the Red Cross in Italy. He left New York in May and arrived in Paris as the city was under bombardment from German artillery. By June, he was at the Italian Front. On his first day in Milan he was sent to the scene of a munitions factory explosion, where rescuers had the grim task of retrieving the remains of women workers who had been blown apart by the blast. He described the incident in DEATH IN THE AFTERNOON, writing, "I remember that after we searched quite thoroughly for the complete dead we collected the fragments. "

On July after delivering chocolate and cigarettes for the men at the front line he was seriously wounded in a mortar attack. Despite his wounds, Hemingway assisted Italian soldiers to safety, for which he later received the Italian Silver Medal for Bravery. He received severe shrapnel wounds to both legs, underwent an immediate operation and spent five days at a field hospital before being transferred to the Red Cross hospital in Milan. He spent six months at the hospital recovering.

During his hospital stay in Milan, the he fell in love with his American Red Cross nurse, Agnes von Kurowsky Stanfield. Hemingway came home to his parents in Oak Park planning to marry Agnes. Three months later he received a "Dear John" letter from Agnes saying that she was engaged to an Italian officer. Hemingway was devastated by the rejection, and armchair psychologists say that Hemingway was so devastated by Agnes's rejection, that in future relationships, he would follow a pattern of abandoning before his partner could abandon him.

He lived for a while with his parents but quickly discovered that war changes one, and you can't just go home again. Not yet twenty, Hemingway wrote, ""When you go to war as a boy you have a great illusion of immortality. Other people get killed; not you . . . Then when you are badly wounded the first time you lose that illusion and you know it can happen to you." He kicked around Illinois and Michigan for a while then took a job writing for the Toronto Star and other writing assignments in Chicago.

He fell in love with Elizabeth Hadley Richardson, nine years his senior. The two were married and took off for Paris. Hadley had some money and Hemingway worked as a foreign correspondent for the Toronto Star. A baby came along and bounced back and forth between Toronto, Paris, Switzerland and Spain. But the marriage didn't last. Hemingway started an affair with the Pauline Pfeiffer who would become wife number two. In the divorce settlement he gave Hadley the royalties to THE SUN ALSO RISES.

With Hadley they went to Key West, Florida and Hemingway discovered fishing and the joys of the Caribbean lifestyle. Pauline's uncle bought the couple a house in Key West with a carriage house, the second floor of which was converted into a writing studio. Its location across the street from the lighthouse made it easy for Hemingway to find after a long night of drinking. In Key West, Hemingway frequented the local bar called Sloppy Joe's which, although still tourist attraction, isn't even in the same location as it was when Hemingway was there. Only the name is the same.

He called Key West home for almost 10 years. Today the Hemingway House is a Key West tourist attraction famed for its six-toed cats. A ship's captain had once given Hemingway a 6-toed cat, and cats being cats ... Today the Hemingway House is one of the few real "cat houses" in Key West, home to about 50 cats, now all spayed and neutered.

Pauline and Ernest headed off on safari in Africa and his books continued to gain attention and critical acclaim. FAIRWELL TO ARMS established Hemingway's stature as a major American writer. During their safari, Hemingway contracted amoebic dysentery and had to be evacuated by plane.

In Key West, Hemingway bought a 38-foot fishing boat in 1934 which he named "Pilar," the nickname of Hemingway's second wife Pauline and also the name of the woman leader of the partisan band in his 1940 novel of the Spanish Civil War, FOR WHOM THE BELL TOLLS. Hemingway used the boat as a fishing boat and just to get away from it all. He visited Bimini, which he loved and where he would spend considerable time, and then eventually discovered and fell in love with Cuba.

Hemingway left the boat to its former hired captain, Gregory Fuentes, said to have been the basis for the character Santiago from THE OLD MAN AND THE SEA as well as Eddie from ISLANDS IN THE SEA. Fuentes eventually donated the boat to the people of Cuba and it has now been beautifully restored and is housed in a structure behind Hemingway's home in Havana.

Twenty years later those fishing adventures on the Pilar would provide inspiration and fodder for THE OLD MAN AND THE SEA. Hemingway was attracted to Bimini by the tales of incredible fishing available in the Gulf Stream and tales of an Atlantic blue marlin weighing over 500 pounds that was caught off Bimini. That fish is said to have inspired THE OLD MAN AND THE SEA.

In 1937 Hemingway went to Spain for a newspaper syndicate to cover the Spanish Civil War along with an American writer and journalist Martha Gellhorn. Hemingway had met Gellhorn in Key West the year before, around the time when things started to sour with his marriage to Pauline. His experience in Spain, like almost every experience in Hemingway's life, would eventually provide inspiration for his novel FOR WHOM THE BELL TOLLS. Hemingway made several trips to Spain covering the war, but when he returned to Key West there wasn't much left of his marriage to Pauline.

In early 1939, Hemingway crossed to Cuba on his boat and lived for a while at the Hotel Ambos Mundos in Havana. Pauline and the children left Key West and Hemingway went to Cuba and was joined by Martha Gellhorn.

When his divorce from Pauline was finalized, Hemingway married wife number three, Martha Gellhorn in Wyoming in November 1940. They returned to Cuba where they had rented "Finca Vigia" or "Lookout Farm," originally a 15-acre [61,000 square meter] property outside of Havana.

Martha Gellhorn inspired him to write his most famous novel, FOR WHOM THE BELL TOLLS. Written in Cuba, Wyoming and Sun Valley where they summered, the book was published in October 1940, sold half a million copies in months and was nominated for a Pulitzer Prize.

Some interesting theories have been suggested about Hemingway, one being that he was a Soviet spy for Russia. Hemingway and Martha traveled to China, then Europe and returned to Cuba before the US declared war. Seeing the deteriorating conditions in Europe, Hemingway convinced the Cuban government to help him refit the *Pilar*, which he intended to use to ambush German submarines off the coast of Cuba, the theory being the Germans would never be suspicious of a guy just out fishing. It was tough duty for a sports fisherman like Hemingway, but "Agent Argo" had his boat outfitted with a Thompson sub machine gun and hand grenades.

From May 1944 to March 1945, Hemingway was in London and Europe. Hemingway was present at the Normandy Landing wearing a head bandage acquired because of a car accident, not combat. Considered "special cargo" he was not allowed ashore, but the landing craft in which he was riding came within sight of Omaha Beach and came under enemy fire. None of the war correspondents were allowed to land, but they never-the-less watched wave after wave of troops going ashore and being cut down. He was present at the liberation of Paris, although not as legend has it, was he first into the city nor did he liberate the

Hemingway at the helm of his yacht the Pilar.

Ritz. He ended up in the hospital with pneumonia and by the time he was released much of the fighting was over. Never-the-less he was awarded a Bronze Star for bravery under fire as the Defense Department so eloquently reported, "through his talent of expression, Mr. Hemingway enabled readers to obtain a vivid picture of the difficulties and triumphs of the front-line soldier and his organization in combat."

When Hemingway first arrived in London, he met Time magazine correspondent Mary Welsh. Meanwhile his wife, Martha, had been forced to cross the Atlantic in a ship filled with explosives because Hemingway refused to help her get a press pass on a plane. When she arrived, she found Hemingway hospitalized from a car accident. Unsympathetic, she told him he was a bully and she was "through, absolutely finished" with the marriage. She returned to Cuba and filed for divorce. It was the end of marriage number three, but Hemingway had already asked Mary Welsh to marry him the third time they met.

This seemed to be a time when Hemingway was happy and satisfied, although it was a frustrating time. Hemingway said he "was out of business as a writer" from 1942 to 1945 during his residence in Cuba. Mary had a difficult pregnancy, there were car accidents and health problems. Hemingway became depressed as his literary friends began to die. He suffered from headaches, high blood pressure, weight problems and eventually diabetes. He worked on various projects but had difficulty completing them.

When you visit Finca Vigia, Hemingway's house in Havana, you will see the famous pool. It's drained now lest a tourist fall in, but it was once the center of life at the house, not just for Hemingway and Martha but for guests as well. The story is that when Ava Gardner stayed here she liked to swim nude in the pool. As Hemingway became more famous the house was always busy with guests. He needed a place to write in private, so he built a tower next to the pool where he could escape and focus on writing. When Ava was visiting, swimming nude in the pool,

Hemingway had a telescope so he could watch from the tower. I have no idea why he just didn't drop his shorts and jump in the pool with Ava.

Hemingway, who had once been disgusted when a Parisian friend allowed his cats to eat from the table, became enamored with cats in Cuba, keeping dozens of them on the property. He famously explained his cat addiction by saying, "One cat just leads to another."

The Hemingways spent their summers in the newly developed Sun Valley, went back to Europe, stayed in Venice awhile and then went back to Africa for a safari. In 1954, while in Africa, Hemingway chartered a sightseeing flight as a Christmas present to Mary. The plane ended up hitting an abandoned utility pole and crashed. They sent a distress call but another plane passing by reported it had seen no survivors. News of Hemingway's death flashed around the world. The next day a bush pilot found the suvivors, bruised, but alive and picked them up. That "rescue" plane caught fire during takeoff, crashed and exploded! Much like his cats with their nine lives, everyone was still alive, but Hemingway suffered serious injuries. Done with flying, they traveled by road to Entebbe where they were met by journalists intending to report on his death. While he recovered, Hemingway got to read his premature obituaries.

In 1954 Hemingway received the Nobel Prize in Literature. Still recovering from the accidents in Africa, he was unable to travel to Stockholm for the banquet, so received the award at home. He had been nominated two times previously and speculated that his near brushes with death had encouraged the committee to finally give him the award. He had sent an acceptance speech that was conveyed to the Nobel Committee by the American ambassador in Stockholm. In gratitude, and in the Cuban tradition, as many Cubans do, Hemingway presented the medal as a gift to Our Lady of Charity.

Living room at Finca Vigia, Hemingway's home outside of Havana.

The famous pool at Hemingway's Cuba home where Ava Gardner swam nude.

Hemingway's medal was displayed at El Cobre along with other gifts that had been presented to the Virgin. The solid gold medal ended up being stolen, but it was recovered and placed in a secure location, so what you see today at El Cobre is just a poster of the medal and the citation. Tom Miller is a great travel writer, who has written about Cuba, is married to a Cuban woman, and has periodically lived in Cuba. He had wanted to see and hold the real medal, so being married to a Cuban, and knowing the Latin American way of life where everyone is interrelated and knows everyone else, he used his inside connections.

Turns out the actual medal isn't at El Cobre, but for safekeeping is kept in the office of the Archbishop of Santiago de Cuba. Again, using his Cuban connections, he traced the medal to the Archbishop's office, and found an ecclesiastical functionary who reached into the bottom drawer of his old Steelcase desk, rummaged around, and came up with the actual gold medal that had been stuck in the drawer for safekeeping!

Hemingway wrote, "Writing, at its best, is a lonely life. Organizations for writers palliate the writer's loneliness but I doubt if they improve his writing. He grows in public stature as he sheds his loneliness and often his work deteriorates. For he does his work alone and if he is a good enough writer he must face eternity, or the lack of it, each day." In this statement you begin to sense the frustration, the agony, the pressure, and the depression.

Always an avid drinker, although not good for his health, Cuba provided Hemingway with great opportunities to hang out and drink. The injuries he had suffered in from the plane crashes in Africa just contributed to his already deteriorating heath. After the plane crashes, Hemingway, who had been "a thinly controlled alcoholic" throughout much of his life, drank more heavily to combat the pain of his injuries. A friend and drinking buddy when he lived in Cuba once told an interviewer, "Ernest said he like Cuba because they had both fishing and fucking there. I believe that had him try out all the houses of prostitution."

There was a very powerful image of Hemingway as a strong, athletic outdoorsman, one of the world's greatest literary giants. Yet the reality was increasingly different from the image. His life style, accidents, illnesses, heavy drinking, and dwindling self-confidence were wearing him down. Hemingway died at 61, still in many ways a "young man," and in his final days in Cuba he was only in his late 50s, and yet increasingly he looked like an old man, like he was old before his time.

He labored under the heavy mantle of success. He had a public that adored him and expected one blockbuster after another. The house in Cuba was overrun with piles of unanswered inquiries and fan mail, and a constant stream of visitors. His creativity was drying up and he needed a change ... he needed to escape.

Hoping to shake off his depression and stimulate his creativity, he did as he had done in the past, he moved, this time from Cuba to Sun Valley, Idaho, an area he had always enjoyed for hunting and fishing. Hemingway had been spending summers in Idaho and it is there that he wrote A MOVEABLE FEAST and the DANGEROUS SUMMER.

Meanwhile things had changed in Cuba. Initially Hemingway apparently remained on easy terms with the Castro government, telling The New York Times he was "delighted" with Castro's overthrow of the dictator Batista. Hemingway's wife claimed the two only met one time and that time "talked about fishing."

There had been a fishing tournament called the Hemingway Tournament and Fidel won, so Hemingway presented him the trophy. The Cubans in Miami all claim that it was a scuba diver who put the winning fish on Fidel's hook ... with lead weights in the belly.

Hemingway stopped in Cuba on the way home from Spain and spent the winter there, but when they learned that Castro was nationalizing property owned by Americans and other foreign nationals they left Cuba on July 25, 1960, never to return, and went to Sun Valley. They left art and manuscripts in a bank vault in Cuba. After the 1961 Bay of Pigs Invasion by the U.S. and the U.S. prohibiting citizens from going to Cuba, Finca Vigia was expropriated by the Cuban government, complete with furnishings and Hemingway's enormous library.

After leaving Cuba for good, Hemingway and Mary moved to a New York apartment, but Hemingway refused to go out increasingly paranoid that the FBI was watching him, which in fact they were. The FBI began surveilling him when during WWII he was using his boat to patrol the waters off Cuba. In the 50s, the FBI had an agent in Havana detailed by J. Edgar Hoover to keep an eye on Hemingway.

With Hemingway teetering on the verge of a complete breakdown, Mary took him to Idaho and later to the Mayo Clinic where he was admitted under his doctor's name. The FBI knew it was Hemingway and later confirmed that he was treated with electroshock 15 times   Researchers have obtained Hemingway's records at the Mayo, which indicate that the combination of medications given to Hemingway may have created the depressive state for which he was being treated.

He was released and returned home to Idaho and one morning Mary found him in the kitchen holding a shotgun.   He was returned to the Sun Valley Hospital and again transferred to the Mayo Clinic for more electroshock treatments then released in late June 1961. Two days later, in the early morning hours of July 2, 1961, Hemingway "unlocked the basement storage room where the guns were kept, took his favorite double-barreled shotgun upstairs, and in the front entrance foyer shot himself." He was 61.

Despite the official finding that Hemingway "had died of a self-inflicted wound to the head," the initial story released to the press said that the death was accidental. Hemingway's behavior during his final years was like that of his father before his father killed himself, and both his sister and brother committed suicide. Some speculate that all had the same genetic disease which led to mental and physical deterioration. The local Catholic priest who conducted the funeral had been told Hemingway's death was accidental. Five years later, Mary Hemingway confirmed that her husband had shot himself.

The Hemingway House in Cuba is in a small, modest suburb of Havana named San Francisco de Paula. After Hemingway's death in 1961, the Cuban government seized the property among other privately-owned properties. The official Cuban government account is that after Hemingway's death, Mary Hemingway deeded the home, complete with furnishings and library, to the Cuban government, which made it into a museum devoted to the author. Mary Hemingway, however, stated that after Hemingway's suicide, the Cuban government contacted her in Idaho and announced that it intended to expropriate the house, along with all real property in Cuba.

After years of neglect, Cuba belatedly realized the importance of the house and the economic tourist potential. The home, claimed to be in danger of collapse, was restored by the Cuban government and reopened to tourists in 2007. "Finca" is just a Spanish name for property and "Vigia" view, so it simply means "house with a view."

The Hemingway cult in Cuba has been carefully cultivated by the government and is aimed primarily at tourism, which, given the dual currency system and the artificially elevated value of the CUC currency which tourists must use, is all very profitable for the government.

Tours sometimes eat at a place in Old Havana called La Bodeguita. On the wall, midst tons of graffiti, in large handwritten letters it says, "My Mojito in La Bodeguita, My Daiquiri in El Florida" two bars where the Hemingway legend says he hung out. Underneath it is the famous signature of Ernest Hemingway. Nice, but the problem is that when Hemingway was here it was just a small, local little grocery store, like a mini-super. It had a little bar, and some of the local artists and writers would visit there. After the Revolution the restaurant wanted to expand their business, and someone jokingly said of Hemingway, "My Mojito in La Bodeguita, My Daquiri in El Florida" so they stuck it on the wall, copied Hemingway's signature, and the little joke grew into a big lie. When the owners confessed to the government tourist board their official response was, "It could help with tourism: just don't write about it in public."

So, the Hemingway Cuban myth grew. Cubans who knew Hemingway point out that he was in many ways a gringo snowbird who liked to winter in Cuba. That he "liked Cubans in the abstract, but not individually." He learned Spanish in Spain and apparently knew all the Spanish bad words in Castilian, not Cuban, Spanish. Friends told him that he should talk to more P&P. When Hemingway asked, "Who's P&P?" They replied, "Prostitutes and peasants" because he didn't really know a lot of Cubans.

When you go to Hemingway's house be prepared for a line, but it's worth it. You cannot go inside but look in through the windows, which sounds a little kinky, but it is actually very nice because you get to see the home without it being cluttered with fellow tourists. Wear a hat, sunscreen, and take along some water.

The restoration is well-done, and you can almost imagine that you are peering into the window, grabbing a quick look, before Mary and Ernest get back home.

[17]The Hotel Ambos Mundos, Havana where Hemingway stayed on the fifth floor.

Milking the legend: La Bodeguita where Hemingway supposedly drank: "My Mojito in La Bodeguita, My Daquiri in El Florida"

With the Embargo, and the collapse of the Soviet Union, the restoration of now government-owned properties, has been slow, even when many of these properties have great potential for tourist income. With the help of historic preservation organizations in the U.S. and others, the restoration and preservation of Finca Vigia has been an ongoing project and has cost almost $1 million U.S. But it is a fascinating, well-done tourist attraction, and worth waiting in line for a chance to look inside Hemingway's life in Cuba.

President Kennedy, although he had never met Hemingway, was a fan of his work. Hemingway was among the American artists, writers, and musicians invited by President and Mrs. Kennedy to attend the 1961 inauguration. But the Hemingway was too ill to travel, as we now know being treated for depression.

When Hemingway died later that year, a large portion of his literary and personal estate remained at Finca Vigia, which he had left during Fidel Castro's revolution, and his papers, manuscripts and some paintings were where Mary had secured them in a bank vault in Havana. Despite a U.S. ban on travel to Cuba, President Kennedy made arrangements for Mary Hemingway to enter Cuba to claim family documents and belongings. While in Cuba, Mrs. Hemingway met with Fidel Castro who allowed her to take her husband's papers and the artwork he collected in exchange for the "donation "of their Finca Vigia home and its remaining belongings to the Cuban people. With Fidel Castro's personal approval, she was able to ship crates of papers and paintings on a shrimp boat from Havana to Tampa.

In 1964 a mutual friend put Mary Hemingway and Jackie Kennedy in contact and Mary offered her husband's collection to the Kennedy Presidential Library and Museum which was being planned as a memorial to the 35th President. The Kennedy Presidential Library and Museum is now the repository for this massive collection of Hemingway's papers and manuscripts.

Mary Walsh Hemingway died in New York in 1986. She was 78.

With Hemingway you have four marriages and what in many ways an epic life that produced a tremendous flow of books and short stories. Yet, despite the success and acclaim, Hemingway would observe, "Writing at its best is a lonely life."

Highlights

There are great advantages to taking a cruise. You know what to expect; you don't have to pack and unpack constantly and have your luggage outside the door by 7:00 a.m., the food is great and safe, you have your own medical staff standing by if needed and they speak your language, you travel with, hopefully, a congenial group of fellow travelers, not tourists, and someone has done all the work of planning, booking, and scheduling. You just get to sit back and enjoy.

There can also be some disadvantages, particularly if you are cruising on a gargantuan ship with thousands of passengers threatening to outnumber the residents of the place you are visiting. That's particularly a risk in Cuba, which is a good argument for taking a small ship to explore Cuba.

I've been in the cruise business for many years and I've seen a great deal of the world on cruise ships. Sometimes it's like going to a grand buffet and just nibbling around the edges without ever really diving into feast. Cruising can sometimes feel like that. The ideal way to see a country is to experience it, to spend time, and to soak up the ambiance and culture. It's unfortunate, but that is not always possible.

Most of the cruises that specifically go to Cuba and are not just making a one-day port stop, go around the island and make multiple stops. Often from the ports you travel inland to experience more of the highlights of Cuba.

The tour buses used in Cuba are some of the best I've experienced, anywhere. They are new, made in China, comfortable and even have working rest rooms and usually are even unlocked so you can use them.

Tour guides in Cuba are generally good. Some are fantastic, but occasionally you get one who must have a relative in some important government position. You'll be surprised to find out that your tour guide may be a doctor or engineer, but working part time as a tour guide, can make more money in a single day than they would make professionally all month! Most ordinary Cubans need to work several jobs to make ends meet.

If you get the idea that things are kind of scripted, they are. This is not a free society. Your guide will tell you that you can ask any questions you want, and they will give you an honest answer that is part of the script. They will try and give you straight answers ... up to a point. But remember, being a guide is a very lucrative job which everyone wants to keep. The bottom line is that the government oversees pretty much everything. Tourism is an important source of revenue, not just for the actual Cubans involved with tourists, but for the government as well. Remember the CUCs that you are required to use are artificially pegged to the U.S. dollar at one to one, but outside of Cuba are worthless, so the government has a hefty take on each foreign currency transaction. For the most part ordinary Cubans use COPs, the Pesos that are worth about four U.S. cents.

But the amazing people of Cuba, the architecture, the history, the culture are more than worth the price of admission! Here are some of the most interesting places, many of which will likely be on your itinerary. Some of these ports are currently on itineraries and others are planned to be available for future voyages.

Cuban tour buses are among the finest. Made in China they have working restrooms.

Cuban guides are generally quite good and since a guide can make in tips in an afternoon what a physician may make in a month, there is good reason to be great at your job!

Casilda

Casilda is a sleepy little waterfront town on the Bay of Casilda that is home to Cuba's small shrimp fishery. An interesting thing about shrimp in Cuba is that it is a food luxury, primarily for tourists, and not easily available or affordable for most ordinary Cubans.

I know Casilda doesn't look very impressive, but in 1519 Hernan Cortez stopped here to recruit men, mostly slaves, with whom to go on to conquer Mexico.

The tiny port facility at Casilda is good for small ships because it offers the easiest and quickest access to Trinidad. It's about a 15-minute ride to Trinidad from Casilda, versus an hour-long, bumpy ride from Cienfuegos to Trinidad.

The other important aspect to Casilda is that it is the nearest town to the Ancon Beach area which is across the Bay. The 2.5-mile-long (4-kilometer) beach has palm trees, turquoise waters, white sand, people in bikinis and three all-inclusive resorts, just the kind of thing that the U.S. government wants to protect U.S. tourists from enjoying! But for Europeans and Canadians escaping winter, it is paradise!

Casilda has dirt roads, a few bed and breakfast homes, dogs sleeping in the street, and the only thing to do is to sample the local beer at a little outdoor bar. Cristal or Bucanero are the tourist beers, priced in CUCs, the tourist currency, and too expensive for most locals. The locals drink Cacique and Mayab, cheaper since they are priced in COPs, the local currency, and with a little less alcohol, somewhat like Coors Light.

Cienfuegos

In Cienfuegos you are docked just a 15-minute walk from the center of town. It's an easy, flat walk, wide streets, low-key, friendly people. Often ships dock here for several days as this can be used for a jumping off point for Trinidad and El Nicho, so you should be able to find some time to go out, walk around town, meet some real folks and have your own, genuine people to people experience. "Hola!" is "Hello!" That and a smile and a friendly attitude is pretty much all you need. Skip happy hour on board, go for an early morning walk before breakfast and enjoy the town waking up, or have dinner in one of the local restaurants.

Cienfuegos, literally means "a hundred fires," but unfortunately has nothing to do with burning sugar cane fields before harvest. It was originally called Fernandia de Jagua, Jagua being the name the Indians used for the area, and Ferdinand being the King of Spain. Later the name was changed to Cienfuegos after the Cuban Governor General at the time, Jose Cienfuegos.

Cienfuegos was founded in 1819 by French settlers from America and Haiti. Many of these were owners of sugar plantations. Those from Haiti had managed to survive the slave riots in Haiti and those from the U.S. who were alarmed by an emerging abolitionist movement, both trying to cope with a rapidly changing world. In 1807 Britain outlawed slave trading and in 1833 outlawed slavery entirely, followed in 1862 by the Emancipation proclamation in the U.S. Spanish Cuba at the time seemed like a good bet because Cuba was still legally and illegally importing slaves until 1886. This influx of French settlers gave a decidedly French provincial feeling to Cienfuegos.

At the time, more sugar was being shipped out of Cienfuegos than any other place in the world, making plantation owners and sugar merchants fabulously wealthy, and you can see evidences of that remaining around Cienfuegos.

On the main square in the center of town is the Teatro Thomas Terry built in 1886 to fulfill the last will and testament of Thomas Terry an unscrupulous sugar factory owner who became wealthy through the slave trade and then became mayor. Maybe this was his way of seeking some atonement after his death. Sarah Bernhardt and Enrico Caruso both performed here in the early 1900s and it remains a beautiful old theater that is still in use today. It cost a few CUCs to get inside but it is worth seeing.

Palacio Ferrer sits on one corner overlooking the Plaza. This was the summer cottage for one of the sugar merchants. These folks had their principal houses in Havana but during the sugar harvest liked to be in Cienfuegos nearer to the action. The main living area was on the second floor and the ground floor was for carriages, servants, company offices, supplies and the like. Caruso stayed here when he performed up the street at the theater. The house is used today for various cultural events.

For me the most stunning "cottage" is out overlooking the harbor. Palacio Valle was built by a sugar merchant, who was then one of the wealthiest men in Cuba. He couldn't quite agree on a single style, so he had his architect combine elements of Gothic, Venetian and neo-Moorish motifs. The three different front towers are intended to symbolize power, religion, and love. Today the building houses a restaurant specializing in seafood

RichardDetrich.com

The beautiful Tomas Terry Theater on the main square, Park Marti, was build 1886-1889,

The Triumphal Arch from 1902 welcomes you to Park Marti the hub of life in Cienfuegos.

and it is open for both lunch and dinner and is only a short cab ride from the pier.

Another grand old structure overlooking the harbor is the Cienfuegos Club built as a yacht club in 1920. It Is another place you might consider for lunch dinner. It gets great reviews for seafood and drinks and is open to the public. If you want to go in and look around during the day, they charge you a CUC.

If you decide to walk into town you will pass another remnant of Cienfuegos sugar history. When the U.S. started buying up Cuban sugar plantations after the Spanish-Cuban-American War, they brought with them the technology and expertise of railroading and built railroads to cart the sugar from fields to factories and then to the ports for shipment abroad. Walking into town you will pass the run-down Parque de Los Locomotoras where they old steam engines from the sugar trains sit decaying away.

At the heart of the city is the Parque Marti in honor of Cuba's national hero who argued and fought for the liberation of Cuba from Spain, the poet and writer, Jose Marti. Marti's best quote is "The only way to be totally free is through education" and that is the basis for Cuba's policy of free education from preschool through university.

Facing the square is a beautiful, red-domed building, which is known as Antiguo Ayuntamiento or "The Old Town Hall." Today it has governmental offices and is not open to the public. Also, on the square is the Cathedral of the Immaculate Conception built 1833-1839, It is well-worth stepping inside if only to appreciate the fantastic French stained-glass windows depicting the Twelve Apostles.

Just off the main square you'll find several broad, pedestrian only streets. The official government stores may have a lot of empty shelves, at least for essentials that people buy, but you'll

The beautiful Old Town Hall just off Plaza Marti in the center of Cienfuegos.

Every town in Cuba has a memorial to the National Hero, Jose Marti. The statue in Cienfuegos is my favorite.

find entrepreneurial capitalism alive and well at individual craft and souvenir street kiosks

When you are walking along the commercial street just off Plaza Marti be sure to stick your head into some of the stores. You'll likely see a big line stretching outside at the store where people get their monthly ration allotment. Things aren't rationed in the sense of their being such a limited supply, although there is, but because the Cuban government to keep people from starving provides everyone with enough food to keep them alive. To claim your government food allotment, you bring a little book called a "ration book" where your allotments are noted. You're not going to do very well on your government food allotment alone. For example, you get thee eggs per person *per month*. Now, knowing that you could have easily gotten a three-egg omelet on the ship, you can imagine how hard life is for many Cubans. Cubans have become very adept at making things work, somehow, some way cobbling things together. Yes, there is a lot of waiting in lines, but ... you can hire people to wait in line for you!

El Cobre

El Cobre can be reached either from the port at Casilda or from Cienfuegos. It is about an hour ride from Cienfuegos, and about 15 minutes from Casilda. It is a beautiful ride and your jaw will drop when you see this beautiful church rising out of the landscape.

Along the way the bus will sometimes stop at a roadside stand where you can buy flowers, preferably sunflowers. Why? Because the Virgin of El Cobre, Nuestra Senora de la Caridad, or "Our Lady of Charity" likes flowers, and if you are going to visit, and have a special request, it's a good idea to bring flowers, yellow flowers.

The Cobre mine the oldest copper mine in the new world operated from 1544 to 1998. The Spanish used slaves and later free colored labor to work the mine. The copper mine was abandoned in the 19th century, then reopened a few times, finally being run by a U.S. company at the start of the 20th century. After the Cuban Revolution it was taken over by the state. In 2001 the mine was closed as no longer profitable and the 325 remaining workers were laid off. The quarry filled with water, which is high in minerals, particularly sulfur. The mine property was given by the government to the church, maybe with the government secretly praying for a Divine miracle of environmental rehabilitation. The church is now the main business of the town.

The Basilica of Our Lady of Charity nestled in the hills above El Cobre.

[18]The Virgin of Charity, El Cobre.

Historically the little mining town became known as El Cobre or, "The Copper" and the church officially and literally in English is called the "Basilica of Our Lady of Charity of the Copper." In Cuba, "El Cobre" refers to the church, to Our Lady of Charity, and to the actual statue of Our Lady. Pilgrims get to the church by climbing on their knees up 254 steps, but not to fear, your tour bus will take you up to the parking lot behind the church. No steps.

The legend is that around 1600, two native Indians, Rodrigo and Juan de Hoyos, along with a ten-year-old slave boy, Juan Moreno, hereafter always referred to as "the three Juans," went to the seacoast to get salt to preserve meat for their town of El Cobre. As they were sailing their little boat across the bay toward home, they ran into a fierce storm that threatened to sink them. The slave boy had an image of the Virgin around his neck and they began to pray for their lives. The waves abated, and the storm stopped, and off in the distance they saw a white object on a board floating toward them. As it came closer they thought it was a bird, then a girl, but when it came closer they realized it was a statue of the Virgin Mary holding the Christ child on her right arm and with a gold cross in her left hand. The statue was fastened to a board with the inscription, "I am the Virgin of Charity." Despite the storm and waves, neither the figure of the Virgin, nor her clothing, was wet.

The statue was brought back to El Cobre but mysteriously would disappear and then reappear and theft, not miraculous behavior, was suspected. Finally, when the statue had again disappeared a little girl had a vision of butterflies and the statue on a hill outside town and when they went to the hill, and voila! there was the statue. And so, in 1826 they built this beautiful church in which to house the statue and where pilgrims could come to pray. In 1916 at the request of the veterans of the War of Independence, Our Lady of Charity was declared the patroness of Cuba by Benedict XV in 1916.

[19]The legend of the Three Juans and the El Cobre Virgen of Charity

As is often the case the legend is far more interesting than the reality. The Virgen of Charity was being venerated in Spain and regarded as the protector of fishermen and seafarers. It appears that an early bishop wanted a statue of the Virgin of Charity and ordered one from Spain. Not as interesting but ... One of the best things I learned in seminary was, "History as a living fact consists not so much in what actually happened, as in what people believe to have happened." That's why in politics you have "spin doctors" who work overtime to craft your perception of reality. So, in this case, the legend is far more interesting and endearing.

Six different popes have endorsed or blessed the statue of the Virgin of Charity and her church, and most recently, Pope Francis became the first Pope to actually visit the church and pray before the statue when he visited Cuba in 2015. The Pope celebrated Mass in the church and even Cuban President Raul Castro was present for Mass.

"El Cobre" as she is known, is the most important and revered item in Cuba. The current incarnation of the statue is of a mulatto Virgin who, although she can be dressed in various colored robes depending on the occasion, is typically dressed in golden yellow. The yellow being *very* significant as you will discover. As the patroness and protector of Cuba, the statue has survived wars, earthquakes, and even the so-called atheistic Communist state. Cubans believe that if they ask the Virgin of Charity for help, comfort and success she will deliver. When the copper mines were working there was a tradition that if you took a little stone of copper with you it would bring you luck. And the tradition was that if your requests were granted you would bring something in gratitude as a gift to the Virgin, not necessarily money, but something.

At the church you have this amazing collection of gifts people have brought to the Virgen in gratitude of gratitude for her h help and for granting their wish. It's an amazing collection of

Inside the Basilica of San Cobre

Pope Francis at El Cobre. Photo: Granma, "The Official Voice of the Communist Party of Cuba Central Committee" and the caption reads, "Army General Raúl Castro Ruz, President of the Councils of State and Ministers, greets Pope Francis before the mass held in honor of Our Lady of Charity of El Cobre." The man to Raul's right is Miguel Diaz-Canel Raul's likely successor.

crutches, academic dissertations, balls and bats, medals, dirt brought back by Cuban soldiers who fought inn African wars, even trimmings from the beards of rebels who were with Fidel in the Sierra Maestro.

One of the most stunning gifts is the Nobel Prize presented to Ernest Hemingway and subsequently presented to the Virgin of Charity at El Cobre.

There are just two problems with El Cobre, one, a theological problem that's plagued the church for centuries, and the other a problem unique to Cuba. The first, theological problem, is the veneration of objects.

In the early days of Christianity, it was thought that simple, uneducated people needed relics of Jesus and saints to inspire their belief and devotion. In "Pillars of The Earth" you remember how important it was for the new cathedral to have the relic of a saint in to bring business to the town and for the cathedral to prosper even if, after the true relic was destroyed in the fire, any old skull was substituted.

This has always been both a bane and blessing to the church. Going all the way back to Thomas Aquinas, the church questioned the practice and theology of venerating relics, but the tradition none-the-less persisted. It is said that there are so many pieces of the true cross floating around that it's enough to rebuild St Peter's. The church resolved that problem with the Pope declaring that the cross had the miraculous power to reproduce itself. There were so many foreskins of Jesus that the church finally declared them all fake and put that relic scheme to rest. So that's a problem with El Cobre and is why Popes, up until Francis, have kind of kept their distance.

The second and larger problem in Cuba is that there are two primary religions in Cuba: Roman Catholicism and the Afro-Cuban religion of Santeria. What you have today in Cuba is the strange melding of aspects of traditional Christianity with traditional African spiritualism. On the surface it would appear that Cuba is predominantly Christian and mostly Catholic, and that is true, but as we mentioned earlier probably 70% of Cubans also practice Santeria. In fact, to be a follower of Santeria you must first be a baptized Catholic. This dual religious practice and commitment has made it uncomfortable for the Roman Catholic Church which has always insisted that it is the true church and hence frowns on mixing faiths.

With acceptance being a hallmark of Francis' papacy, perhaps his visit to El Cobre indicates that he is thinking more along the lines of Luis del Castillo, an 80-year-old retired Uruguayan bishop, who now teaches at the seminary in Santiago de Cuba. "From the Church there is no aggressive opposition to Santeria," he said. "For us to be able to teach about the Bible and make known the teachings of Jesus Christ is enough."

The fact is that many, if not most, of those who come to El Cobre are there on a dual mission, both to pay honor and respect to the Virgin of Charity and also to honor to Santeria orisha Oshun whose color is ... you got it ... yellow. That's the reason for all the yellow sunflowers. A visit to El Cobre and a supplication to the Virgin is a two-for-one. At the same time, they are petitioning both the Virgin and Oshun.

Even if you are not religious, you will enjoy your visit to El Cobre. A highlight is often our visit is this tiny community's steel band music program.

Steel band community project in the tiny town of El Cobre.

Real people to people interaction with locals outside the community steel band project in El Cobre.

El Nicho

El Nicho natural reserve is one of the gems in the Escambray Mountains, a mountain range in the central region of Cuba stretching across the provinces of Sancti Spirtus, Cienfuegos and Villa Clara. This is some of the most beautiful rainforest in Cuba.

Usually driving from the port in Cienfuegos, along the way you pass some interesting little villages that will give opportunity to see some of the *real* Cuba, off the standard tourist routes. Cumanayagua, for example, was inhabited by Indigenous Taino people when the Spanish arrived at the island. The name comes from the Taino and some scholars believe it means "The place filled with flowers of Royal Palms."

Coffee grows best in high mountain areas that get lots of rain and preferably in volcanic soil. There was a time when coffee was an important export crop for Cuba, but now Cuban coffee is grown for local consumption. On the way to El Nicho you will pass through Cumanayagua, a sleepy mountain town with a population of about 50,000 people, where they raise citrus and coffee for mostly national consumption.

The Gran Parque Natural Topes de Collantes is a forested park that extends across the Sierra Escambray mountain range in Central Cuba. A series of freshwater cascades has become a highlight for locals and visitors with its beautiful views of Central Cuba and the valley below.

This is home to El Nicho waterfalls, one of the most spectacular series of cascades, with one cascade after another in this natural wonderland of waterfalls. Take along your bathing suit, but remember, although the air can be hot, the water in the waterfall is coming down from high in the mountains, so it provides opportunity for a cool and refreshing dip.

El Nico Reserve waterfalls in Sierra del Escambray Mountains.

Guantanamo

Guantanamo is a city in Cuba. But for many U.S. Americans "Guantanamo" isn't the city in Cuba, but the U.S. Naval Base at Guantanamo Bay.

You can get to the Cuban town of Guantanamo, but you cannot get to the U.S. Naval Base at Guantanamo Bay from Cuba. Even American Citizens are not permitted, well unless that is they take a very circuitous route, which is the route Tom Miller took to visit U.S. Naval Base at Guantanamo Bay from Cuba.

Miller, a U.S. citizen, married to a Cuban, has family in Cuba and as a travel writer focusing on Cuba so he has been back and forth. He'd been to the Cuban town of Guantanamo and, looked over the fence at the U.S. Naval Base, but as a U.S. citizen ... well, let him tell it.

"Theoretically, to get to the base from Cuba, should be simple; head south from the city of Guantanamo until you reach the northern gate, knock three times, and enter. That's essentially how it was until relations broke down in the early 1960s. To travel now from Guantanamo, Cuba, to the U.S. Navy Base, one must drive seventy-five kilometers west [47 miles] to Santiago de Cuba, take Cubana Airlines 590 miles [950 kilometers] northwest to Havana, hope on the daily charter northwest 225 miles [362 kilometers] to Miami, fly north 979 miles [1,575 kilometers] to Norfolk, Virginia, get approval from the Navy, and take one of its twice-weekly charters out of Norfolk 1,200 miles [1,931 kilometers] southeast to the base. U.S. military planes can't fly over Cuba proper, so pilots have to dog-leg sharply around the country's southeast coast and angle in for a tense, peacetime landing. After this . . . one-way trip, you are virtually face-to-face with where you were four days earlier."[20]

Now I grant you since the Obama reset on Cuba, American Airlines now flies direct to Miami from Cuba on scheduled flights, so it's a bit easier, but you still must go, almost "by way of China," to get from Guantanamo, Cuba to the U.S. Naval Base at Guantanamo Bay, Cuba, at least if you are a U.S. citizen with your tax dollars and paying for the base. Makes you wonder what they are trying to hide.

If your ship is sailing around Cuba, you'll be 12 miles [19 kilometers] off the coast, probably at night, when you pass Guantanamo Bay and about all you will see is some red lights from the airfield and a concentrated mass of white lights, presumably those of the presently operating Camp Delta prison complex.

The right for the U.S. to have a U.S. Naval Base in the sovereign territory of Cuba goes back to the Platt Amendment that was forced on Cuba as a condition of removing U.S. troops after the Spanish-Cuban-American War. At the time the U.S. was angling for a Canal across Panama and wanted a naval base in Cuba, the "key to the Caribbean," in order to protect U.S. interests in Panama. This agreement was forced on Cuba and then followed up with something called the 1903 Treaty of Relations, spelling out the U.S. right to naval bases in Cuba.

The U.S. closed 22 military bases in Panama and gave the Canal back to Panama in 2000 for two reasons. First, colonialism was out. There was no good reason for the U.S. to maintain a colony in the sovereign nation of Panama. Second, all those 22 bases were obsolete. The way of waging war had changed. The obsolete bases and all the vested interests that had a piece of the pie were wasting the money of U.S. taxpayers.

The same two reasons apply today in Cuba to the U.S. Naval Base at Guantanamo. There is no reason, other than to continue to provoke Cuba, for the U.S. to maintain an unwanted a U.S. colony, complete with a McDonald's, in sovereign Cuban territory. Second, the base at Guantanamo was built to protect U.S. interests when it occupied Panama and owned the Panama Canal, all of which is now Panama's and has been for 18 years. An obsolete base continues to waste more U.S. taxpayer money than Panama ever did!

Then there is the Cuban town of Guantanamo founded in 1796 by French fleeing the slave rebellion in Haiti. The song "Guantanamera" was originally written in Guantanamo, and later verses by Jose Marti were added. Today the town has a population of around 200,000 and produces sugar and cotton which are shipped from the nearby port town of Caimanera which lies between the U.S. base and the town of Guantanamo. The town of Guantanamo really doesn't have any significant touristic claim to fame.

Prior to the Castro Revolution almost three thousand people from Caimanera worked on the U.S. base and the military freely patronized local bars and prostitutes. After the Revolution only those who already worked on the base could continue, and the town was placed off-limits to Cubans unless they lived there are had special permission because of its proximity to the base. The last two Cuban workers retired in 2010 and now all menial work on the base is done mostly by Puerto Ricans.

[21]Obama tried, and failed, to close the obsolete U.S. Naval Base at Guantanamo. According to CNN, ACLU *and* FOX the prison facility alone costs U.S. taxpayers $11 million per year *per inmate*.

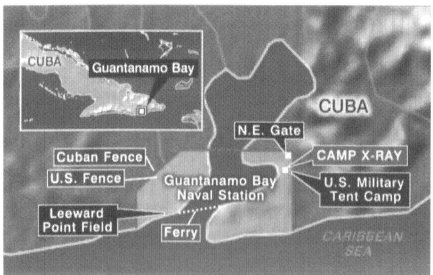

[22]All this obsolete and originally built to protect the U.S. Panama Canal and U.S. Canal Zone which haven't existed since 2000.

Havana

Sailing into Havana Harbor is a thrill for most U.S. Americans who have been denied this privilege by our own government for over 50 years. Sailing past the lighthouse at the fortress, Castillo del Morro, or "Castle of The Hill," is a memorable moment. The Harbor of San Juan was a key stopover point for ships carrying the treasure of the New World, gold, silver, gems, hardwoods, from Panama and Cartagena, back home to Spain. The fort was intended to keep the pirates at bay while the ships re-provisioned for the long journey across the Atlantic back to Spain.

Be up on deck when you sail in! You will you see the Old historic city of Havana, a UNESCO World Heritage site, laid out before you. Ahead is the star-shaped Castillo de la Real Fuerza, or "Castle of the Royal Force," and the building in the back that vaguely resembles the U.S. Capitol building is in fact the old Capitol building of Cuba built back in 1929. Stretching out along the seawall is Havana's famous seaside promenade, the Malecon.

Ships dock right in downtown in the "La Havana Vieja" or the old, historic city which is a UNESCO World Heritage site. It's all right there! Just a few blocks from the dock and in easy walking distance for many is Plaza Vieja, the beautiful, old original plaza, now wonderfully restored.

Don't miss the sail in to Havana Harbor sailing past El Morro fort.

Just a block or so away from the dock is the beautifully restored Plaza Vieja.

And despite some run down and poor areas, you find Havana, and Cuba as a whole, to be a safe place to walk around. Though not always visible, there are state security police everywhere.

The first thing you will do when you get off the ship is go into the beautifully restored terminal where you will go through immigration.   When you get through immigration you want to immediately walk to the opposite end and get in line to change money into CUCs.

Cuba uses two currencies: the Cuban peso (CUP) and the Cuban convertible peso (CUC) are both legal tender. The CUC, or "Kook" as it is pronounced in Spanish, is used by tourists and is pegged one to one to the US dollar. The CUP or "Koop," again Spanish pronunciation, is the currency used by locals. They are not of equal value. While 1 CUC equals $1 U.S., local CUP is only worth about 4 US cents if it could be changed, which it cannot. Neither currency can be changed outside of Cuba. As a tourist you will deal in CUCs and because of the Embargo you cannot use credit cards issued by U.S. banks.

If this sounds rather "kooky" it is! Foreign currency can only be changed at the government change bureaus. You will be charged a 3% transaction fee. In addition, if you are changing U.S. dollars you will be charged an additional 10% penalty. So, if you give them $100 U.S. you will get $87 U.S. worth of CUCs. Yes, it is a rip off, but that's the way it is, so accept it and get on with it.

Caution: the two currencies are both called "peso" just to add to the confusion, but *the two currencies look different.* If you are due change look at the bills, and make sure you are getting the right bills in change. *The CUCs, the currency you use, has pictures of monuments. The CUPs, the currency you don't want, ha pictures of people.*

If you have extra CUCs at the end of your cruise you can change them one to one, with no additional charge, back into U.S. dollars at the government exchange offices at the pier.

You will need CUCs for purchasing souvenirs, rum, and cigars, eating, or riding Yank Tank taxis independently, and for gratuities to guides. With most cruise lines when you are an excursion the cost of lunches, and tips at the restaurants used on the tours, are covered by the ship.

Although some guides are happy to accept tips in CUCs or U.S. dollars, when they attempt to change the U.S. money they too are charged the fees, and honestly the tips *are* their income.

Don't worry, you will see old cars, tons of them in Havana and elsewhere. When the U.S. embargoed Cuba in 1957 it was no longer possible to import U.S. cars, so Cuban ingenuity has kept these old cars running, many of them beautifully maintained. Locally they are called Yank Tanks, and most are taxis, the nicest ones for tourists, and the older, more beat-up ones for locals. There are over 60,000 of these on the road in Cuba. Unfortunately, due to the U.S. Embargo, many of the cars have been kept running with parts, even engines, from the old Soviet Union.

Whenever we're you are ashore on tours you will have great meals, usually in one of the local Paladares, or house restaurants that sprang up during the "special period" when as a matter of survival Cuba encouraged this kind of capitalistic entrepreneurialism. An FYI, be gracious, even if something isn't exactly up to your expectations since you are enjoying the best available and, in many cases, the kind of food unavailable to ordinary Cubans. Uncomfortable? At times yes, but understand that Cuba is different, which is why we came.

If you are looking to buy cigars or rum: don't buy it on the street. There is a wide variance in the quality of cigars. On the street you are buying seconds or thirds or just plain rejects. This is NOT St Thomas, St Martin or the other big cruise ports. There are no "preferred stores" and the cruise line isn't getting a kick back. And you don't have to traipse store to store looking to save money because the prices are all the same and are set by the government.

The Plaza de la Revolucion is a giant parade ground created by the dictator Batista in 1959 and known as Plaza Civica until Castro's Revolution. The towering monument is to Jose Marti the national hero of Cuba. The Plaza can hold more than a million people and has been used for speeches by Fidel, national military parades, and in 2012 for an outdoor mass by Pope Benedict. Most days it's a place to show off your car.

Don't miss at least walking by the beautiful Art Deco Bacardi Building, headquarters of Bacardi Rum until, after the Castro Revolution, they fled Cuba. Nearby is the old Cuban Capitol building, built in the `1920s and the dome resembling the U.S. Capitol building and the domed capitols of many U.S. States. Like many of the beautiful old buildings in Havana, it is under renovation and covered in scaffolding. Today it houses the Ministries of Science, Technology and the Environment. In the rotunda is a gigantic giant statue of the Republic in bronze covered with 22 carat gold. It is the third largest statue in the world.

The beautiful Plaza de la Catedral is one of the highlights of a walking tour of the old city. The Cathedral of St Christopher was constructed by the Franciscans in 1777. The Cathedral once held the remains of Christopher Columbus but when the Spanish were defeated in the war of 1898 they stole Columbus and took him back to Spain. That lady dressed all in white with a red flower on her hand and a giant cigar in her mouth who poses for pictures with tourists on a good day can take home in a single afternoon, under the table and tax

Riding in one of the old Yank Tank taxi cabs

Fantastic Spanish architecture, old cars and welcoming people: it doesn't get any better than this.

free, almost what a Cuban doctor makes in a month. Think about it!

My Cuban exile friends, who left all to escape to freedom in the U.S., will point out that most of the beautiful architecture in Havana was either built by the Spanish or constructed before Castro's revolution, and post-Revolution a lot has just been left to decay. One old building a day collapses in Havana ... just falls down! What my friends say is partly true. But you have a tiny Caribbean island nation, completely cut off by the geopolitical climate, whose fortunes really kept going from bad to worse, and who only managed to survive by sheer determination, if not because of the new government, despite it. In Havana today, buoyed by European and Canadian tourism, and now just a trickle of cruise ships from the U.S., Cuba is working hard to restore and save whatever architecturally significant buildings that remain. That renovation effort by the way is funded by all the government run tourist companies we are not allowed to use, so now, in no way are we helping directly to restore these marvelous but crumbling old buildings. But then there *is* that 10% penalty they charged when you changed your U.S. money into CUCs.

Cuba is, as it always has been, a work in progress and they know it. You are lucky to make this voyage, both while you can, and before all the giant cruise ships arrive and turn Havana into another St Thomas or Nassau.

What was once the Presidential Palace, where Batista lived until he fled, is now the Museum of the Revolution. Out in back in a glass pavilion is Granma, the famous leaky boat that brought Castro and his inner circle back from exile in Mexico to launch the Revolution. There are also parts of U.S. planes that were downed during the failed U.S. Bay of Pigs Invasion and the Catering Truck in which Castro's men attempted to sneak into the Presidential Palace.

I couldn't resist these kids, delighted in different ways by the parade of performers on stilts in Plaza Viejo. I was doing my own people to people exploration, chatting with their teacher who had brought his students on a field trip.

The lady telling your fortune in front of the Cathedral can make in a single afternoon more than a physician makes in a month.

Havana's famous seaside promenade, the Malecon, also known as the "world's largest sofa," because it is here in the cool of the night all of Cuba gathers to socialize, romance, play music, visit with one another and celebrate life.

One of the highlights for many ships visiting Havana is the fabulous Tropicana night club show. The show starts at 10:00 p.m. and lasts almost to midnight and I know for many it means staying up late, but, heck, we're adults! We can do whatever we want! And being Latin America, these folks operate on a different time schedule. Yes, there are feathers, skimpy outfits, and rum ... included by the way ... but the show is really the story of Cuban culture as told through a progression of dance and music. This is probably a bigger production that you've ever seen anywhere, bigger than anything on ships, even bigger than Vegas. So, get wild and crazy and stay up! And guys, keep your pants on ... well, maybe a better way to phrase it is, wear long pants, no shorts.

In the current political climate, it's important to note these are not "cruises" but educational people to people voyages. Even although there are no grades or report cards, attendance is expected and yes, they do take attendance. But, as I'm sure you already know, travel is one of the world's greatest educational adventures. Education can be *fun* despite the current flurry of regulations from politicians... the same guys who apparently are against regulations. Go figure!

Your cruise is going to keep you very busy enjoying the sights, sounds, smells and rhythm of Cuba. For U.S. citizens these are billed as a people to people tours. The original Obama Cuba policy has been modified by Trump and is now the Trump policy. It is more-or-less the same with a few big buts ... Never-the-less, after you've fulfilled your obligation to take the educational adventures ashore, I would encourage you, if you can do it, and if you can possibly find the time ...

even if it means skipping happy hour ... to go out and walk around town. Meet some real Cubans, since this is, after all, supposed to be a people to people experience.

Havana is a feast of sights, sounds, welcoming people, and fascinating experiences.

Holguin

It was here that Columbus landed in 1492, calling the area the most beautiful that he had ever seen. Holguin was founded as San Isidoro de Holguín in 1545 by Garcia Holguin, a Spanish military officer. Today it is Cuba's fourth largest city with a population of about 240,000. The brewery Cerveceria Bucanero that makes three popular brands of Cuban beer - Bucanero, Cristal and Mayabe,- is in Holguin.

Europeans and Canadians have been flocking to Cuba for twenty years and European and Canadian companies have been investing in Cuban tourist facilities. The U.S. is the late arrival to the party and has yet to really relax, have a drink and start to party. Holguin is "Canada South" for Canadians eager to escape winter on relatively inexpensive charter flights and tour packages. There are two Canadian consulates in Holguin and it is one of the most popular Cuban destination for sun-starved Canadians. Of course, Canadian credit cards are accepted, except for those issued by U.S. banks because of the U.S. Embargo. Canadians, and everyone else but U.S. citizens, can enjoy the beaches and resort life of Cuba, and especially the area around Holguin.

The outdated, tit for tat, U.S. Embargo and prohibitions, plus the Trump roll-back of the Obama attempts to normalize relations with Cuba, means that the U.S. denies its citizens the freedom to travel to Cuba and enjoy everything that Cuba offers. But, at

²³Hill of The Cross, overlooking Holguin.

²⁴Holguin Town Hall. Photo: Anton Zelenov

least for now, you can enjoy Cuba and Holguin on people to people educational tours monitored by the U.S. Treasury Department, but … no beach.

There was a time when street organs were a common form of public entertainment. Organs were built in Holguin, Cuba and some of these Cuban-built instruments ended up in Europe. They were real pipe organs but small enough to be pushed or pulled around. Some were highly decorated with carvings and various colors. They were called "barrel" organs because the music was encoded into a barrel using metal pins and staples. d Today in Holguin you can tour the only remaining mechanical music-organ factory in Cuba which produces only about six organs per year.

Humboldt National Park

The park is named after Alejandro de Humboldt (1769-1859), a German scientist, naturalist, geographer and explorer who travelled extensively in Latin America between 1799 and 1804 exploring and describing his observations from a modern scientific point of view. He studied Cuba from 1800 to 1801 and then he returned for four months in 1804. He is sometimes referred to as the "second discoverer of Cuba" for the research he conducted. Humboldt was one of the first to theorize that the continents had once been joined together, and the Humboldt Current is named after him.

The Alejandro de Humboldt National Park became a UNESCO World Heritage Site in 1991. The area is the most humid in Cuba and has a high biodiversity including 28 endemic plant species, parrots, lizards, hummingbirds, and the endangered Cuban solendon, a rat or shrew-like mammal with venomous saliva that is endemic to Cuba.

Beautiful, brightly colored Cuban land snails, or Polymita picta are endemic to Cuba and found in the park. They have been called the world's most beautiful snail shell and as a result have been collected and used for jewelry and decoration, so are now an endangered and protected species. Look and enjoy but don't take.

German scientist Alejandro de Humboldt for whom the park is named.

[25]Brightly colored Cuban land snails found in Humboldt National Park.

Isla de Juvetud

When Columbus stopped on his second voyage, he named the island La Evangelista, "the evangelist," and claimed the island for Spain. Later it was known as Isla de Cotorras "Isle of the Parrots" and even Isla de Tesoros, 'Treasure Island." Then it became "The Isle of Pines" until 1978 when it was renamed Isla de Juvetud ("The Isle of Youth") by Fidel Castro, fulfilling a promise he made to honor youth for their work in having "revolutionized the natural environment."

As to the name Treasure Island, there were in fact pirates who hung out on and around the island, and both Robert Louis Stevenson in the book TREASURE ISLAND and J. M Barrie in PETER PAM used stories of the island and its history in their writings.

The English name Isle of Pines was not accidental. After the Spanish-Cuban-American War, the terms of the 1898 Treaty of Paris gave the U.S. Cuba. After forcing Cuba to accept the Platt Amendment and withdrawing from Cuba, control of the island was debated for two decades. In 1925, although 95% of the island was owned by U.S. interests, the U.S. finally ceded control of the island to Cuba.

The infamous Modelo prison, constructed by the dictator Machado for political prisoners and later used by Batista, that

26Modelo Prison on the Isle of Pines where Fidel was held prisoner.

27Interior of one of the units at Modelo Prison where Fidel was in prison. The guards we in the central tower so they had no contact with the prisoners.

Fidel was imprisoned, following his capture by Batista's forces after the landing of the Granma. The prison, modeled after one in Joliet, Illinois, is no longer used and today is a museum where you can visit the cell where Castro was held and where he planned his revolution.

Mantanzas

Matanzas was founded in 1693 on the bay of the same name by 30 families from the Canary Islands and became a major area for sugar production, importing slaves to do the work. By 1841 almost 63% of the town's population were slaves. Today the town has a population of around 150,000, still is an important sugar port, and has a rich Afro-Cuban heritage.

Because the town spans three rivers with 17 bridges it has acquired the nicknames of both the "Venice of Cuba" and the "City of Bridges." It has also been called "The Athens of Cuba" because it had in the 19th century the artistic and cultural life of the town was more important than that of Havana. The Sauto Theater, is still one of the city's major attractions.

The town's pharmacist, Ambrosio de la Concepcion Santo, was famous for having developed a lotion that cured Queen Isabella II of Spain of a skin disease. One of the highlights of the city is the Museo Farmaceutico de Matanzas, which was an actual working pharmacy begun in 1882 and turned into a museum in 1964. Shelves are lined with porcelain vases and bottles, it has a library of books on pharmacy, medicine, botany and a historical collection of prescriptions and cures.

The Hershey company, yes that one, had a big sugar factory here, and to connect factory, fields and workers in 1916 developed an electric train that is still in operation today, known as the Hershey Train.

[28]Matanzas Pharmaceutical Museum

[29]The Hershey Electric Train in Matanzas.

Maria la Gorda

"Fat Maria" was abducted by pirates in Venezuela and then abandoned on the island by the pirates. To survive she began servicing the pirates who passed by hungry to sample plump Maria. Located on the end of the western most peninsula of Cuba in the Guanahacabibes Reserve, there is almost nothing here but spectacular reefs and a very unique biosystem. The entire peninsula is a National Park and UNESCO Bioreserve.

The peninsula was one of the last refuges of the Indigenous Taino who fled from the Spanish conquerors and has over 140 archeological sites.

In 1960 as relations with the U.S. deteriorated, forces under the direction of Che Guevara were stationed here to protect Cuba from possible U.S. invasion

In 1961 Cuba cracked down on people it considered moral degenerates, prostitutes, pimps and homosexuals, and sent them to labor camps in what is today the national park to be re-educated.

The diving and snorkeling here is some of the best in the Caribbean. The beaches are beautiful, but, be forewarned, douse yourself in bug spray. Maria la Gorda is known for bugs and mosquitos. The best time on the beach is early to midafternoon. Mornings and late afternoon are the times when the bugs and no-see-ums are worse. Always sit on a towel and never directly on the sand. The sunsets are spectacular if you are sitting on the deck of your ship sailing away. If you are sitting on the beach when the sun sets – good luck! You may be eaten alive by the bugs.

[30]Warm azure water, white sand, palm trees ... everything you'd hope for on Maria la Gorda but watch out for the mosquitos and no-see-ums.

[31]Maria la Gorda offers fantastic snorkeling and diving.

Santiago de Cuba

Eastern Cuba, or "El Oriente" as it is called, is very different from the rest of Cuba. It is here that Columbus stopped on his third voyage leaving behind sugar cane. It is a beautiful area, and because it is the closest point to the island of Hispaniola, today Haiti and the Dominican Republic, Eastern Cuba has a distinct Afro-Cuban heritage and flavor.

Santiago has a spectacular, sheltered harbor guarded at the entrance by another fort also named El Morro. You'll want to be out on deck to enjoy the sail in even if it is before breakfast. Because of its near perfect harbor, Santiago de Cuba has long been the second most important city in Cuba, the second largest, and the second most important port.

The name Santiago is derived from an ancient common form of Latin for Saint James. In addition to Santiago de Cuba there are four other well-known places named Santiago: Santiago, Chile; Santiago, Philippines; Santiago de Compostela, Spain; and Santiago de los Caballeros, Dominican Republic.

Ships dock right in town and the little port is very low key. Getting through immigration is usually quick and easy and these are the friendliest immigration folks I've encountered anywhere. There is a little kiosk to change money right after immigration. It's about a 20-minute walk from the pier into town, up a slight grade.

The magnificent Catedral de la Asuncion overlooking Parque Cespedes in Santiago de Cuba.

Castillo del Morro at the entrance to Santiago Bay was designed in 1637 to defend against pirates and is a UNESCO World Heritage site.

If you walk out of the tiny port area, past the old taxis, past the place to change money, between the buildings, outside of the port, you'll find an old tower in the center of the street. Turn left, away from the tower and walk a block down to a beautiful pink building. Turn right on Calle Jose Antonio Saco, a delightful street that eventually becomes a main shopping street, but before it does, you'll find a great center of little independent, capitalistic shops with vendors selling arts and crafts and artwork. It's just a few blocks up on the left side of the street, an easy walk for many from the ship.

It was here in El Oriente that Castro was born, here where he launched his audacious attack on Batista's Moncado barracks, here he landed in the leaky old yacht Granma, here that he fled into the mountains to plan his Revolution, and here where he is laid to rest.

Just outside the historic town center is the Plaza de la Revolucion. Here is a striking monument of 23 machete blades representing the farmers and peasants who fought in the Revolution. There is a giant statue of General Jose Antonio Maceo, nicknamed "The Great Lion," who fought in Cuba's wars for liberation from Spain.   Maceo also earned the nickname "The Bronze Titan," partly because he was dark-skinned, and partly because he seemed invincible leading his men into 500 battles and being wounded 25 times.

Sometimes tours go to a park called Baconao, now designated a UNESCO biosphere reserve, although it contains a kitschy "Valle de Prehistoria," a children's park featuring decaying life-size cement models of dinosaurs. That tour continues to visit the Siboney farm house, significant because it was here that the rebels stayed the night before they attacked the Moncado barracks in town. In revenge Batista's troops shot up the farm house and you can still see the bullet holes.

As you make your way along the road to the Siboney farm house you'll see periodic monuments along the road, generally not very pretentious. When rebels killed some of Batista's men, in revenge he had rounded up townspeople, men, women and teenagers, stuck them on a truck and drove down the road throwing them off along the way and shooting them. All these monuments along the way commemorate the lives of those martyrs who were killed in what came to be called Batista's "Operation Christmas Present."

There is one thing we all have in common, no matter how powerful or rich we may be, no matter how celebrated or detested, we all die. At the Historic National Cemetery, known as Cementeria de Santa Ifigenia, you will see the graves of Cuba's national heroes, including the relatively simple tomb of Fidel Castro. At his design it is shaped as a seed of corn, and the inscription reads simply "Fidel." The changing of the guard ceremony is primarily to honor of Fidel, but Cuba's national hero, the poet Jose Marti, who is in the grand mausoleum next to Fidel. The black and red July 26 flags fly over the graves of those who fought with Fidel in the Sierra Maestro mountains.

You'll want to be up on deck when we sail in and out of Santiago Harbor because high on the hill, overlooking and protecting the harbor, is the magnificent Castillo del Morro, more formally San Pedro de la Roca del Morro fort, a UNESCO World Heritage site. The fort was built to protect the city from pirates. Construction began in 1638 and it housed as many as 600 soldiers. The Fort has been wonderfully preserved and restored and you can walk around as much as you want, climbing stairs and walls, or if climbing is not your thing, you can just walk around the top and get great views of this monumental structure.

The main Plaza is just a few blocks away from the main shopping street. The Plaza is still the center of life in Santiago de Cuba and is surrounded by half a dozen museums and numerous houses under renovation. The white building is the Town Hall, built in 1950 but according to a long-lost 18th century design for a town hall that was never built. Castro gave his first speech to the Cuban people from the central balcony in 1959. The park is named after one of the founding fathers, Carlos Manuel Cespedes, who gave the first cry for freedom for Cuba to rebel against Spanish rule.

On the opposite side of the Plaza is the Cathedral of the Assumption with a magnificent balcony. To get inside the church just walk around to either of the side streets where there are steps up to the balcony and main entrance. Except for a giant painting of the Virgin on the ceiling, the inside is rather ordinary, so if you don't want to climb up the steps to get inside, you're not missing much except for the view from the balcony outside.

Facing the square is the oldest house in Cuba, the house of Diego Velazquez, the first governor, constructed 1516-1530, and beautifully restored in 1965. It is open as a museum which is fantastic and a not-to-miss attraction in Santiago de Cuba. It costs a couple of COCs to get in but is well worth it. If your tour doesn't include visiting inside the house, walk up to the Plaza from the ship and pay a visit on your own.

People to people experiences vary from visiting a pottery workshop cooperative in an old home that was abandoned when the owners fled Cuba, to a fantastic choral group.

U.S. visitors are always interested in visiting San Juan Hill that was the scene of the bloodiest battle in the Spanish-Cuba-American War, known for the victory over the Spanish defenders by two companies of "Buffalo Soldiers" (African-American troops) and Theodore Roosevelt's Rough Riders. Monuments from various U.S. states and from Spain dot the hilltop and the view over the country side.

Your guides will probably tell you that the famous painting of Teddy Roosevelt leading the charge up San Juan Hill on horseback was more PR and artistic liberty than historical fact. By the time of San Juan Hill, Cuba had been so punished by the cruel Spanish occupation that almost all the horses had been

The Casa de Diego Velazquez off the main Plaza Cespedes was built 1516-1530 and is considered the oldest building in Cuba.

San Juan Hill site of a decisive battle in the Spanish-Cuban-American War.

eaten. It took some doing to find the horse for the famous picture of Roosevelt on horseback.

If the ship is overnight in Santiago frequently there is a night out enjoying the entertainment. Popular spots are a great little Jazz Club Iris, Trova House club specializing in Afro-Cuban music, or the bar atop the Hotel Casa Granda, a bar described by Graham Green in "Our Man in Havana" as a place where spies hung out.

Santiago is the hottest place in Cuba, so at night the squares and parks really come alive when everyone is out enjoying the cool evening. The center for a lot of entertainment is Plaza de Marte, the third largest plaza in Cuba, laid out in the 19th Century. A 65-foot [20 meter] column in the center celebrates Cuban independence. Importantly, since Internet is relatively new in Cuba, Plaza de Marte is an Internet Hot Spot. Now people, instead of actually talking to each other, can now text each other.

One of the most famous exports of Santiago was musician and actor Desi Arnaz, who probably did more than anyone else to create the U.S. American stereotype of Cubans. His father was Santiago's youngest mayor and served in the Cuban House of Representatives. His maternal grandfather was an executive at Bacardi. His father was an ardent supporter of the dictator Gerardo Machado and when Machado was driven out in 1933 his father was jailed, and their property seized. At that time, they fled to Miami where Desi went to Catholic high school. After high school he started a band, landed a lead in a Broadway musical, went on to Hollywood where he met Lucile Ball ... and the rest is history.

Trinidad

Trinidad is kind of a town that time forgot. A long period of isolation from the 1850s to the 1950s protected the town from development and modernization and the original layout and many of the buildings have been left unchanged. In 1988 the historic old town was declared a UNESCO World Heritage site.

The city was founded in 1514 and from the 17th to 19th centuries, the city was a major center for trade in sugar and slaves. Today as a tourist attraction in Cuba Trinidad is second only to Havana. Around every corner are delightful old Spanish colonial homes and structures.

Without air conditioning it was important to be able to leave your windows wide open, day and night. To keep out animals and thieves, Spanish architecture in the Americas featured iron grills over the windows, often with shutters behind them for privacy but which still could allow air flow. In Trinidad these grills had typically had additional decoration on top, and sometimes also at the bottom, giving them the name "birdcage grills."

The streets in Trinidad are paved with cobble stones, not the neatly cut stone blocks like many old streets in Europe, but these are actual river rocks, variously shaped and very

The old historical center of Trinidad is a wonderfully preserved UNESCO World Heritage site.

Uneven cobblestone streets are part of the historical charm but make it difficult for people with walking limitations.

uneven. It's one of the things that makes Trinidad special and preserves the history. However, Trinidad is a walking tour and in no sense of the word is Trinidad ADA (Americans with Disability Act) accessible. Tour buses are not allowed in the central, historic area. If you have walking difficulties the uneven cobblestones can be challenging. Walkers and scooters ... maybe. Wheelchairs, no way. Unfortunately, not every tour is for everybody, so you need to know your body and respect your limitations.

Typically, the tours will stop at one of several artist studios and a pottery shop. Part of the people to people focus is to meet various Cuban artisans and musicians.

The Iglesias y Convento de San Francisco, originally built by the Franciscans in 1730, is in the beautiful historic center of the old town. Only the tower remains from the original structure. In 1895 the convent became a garrison for the Spanish army. It was a school until 1984 when it became the Museo de la Lucha Contra Bandidos, literally "Museum of the fight against bandits." The museum focuses on the struggle against the "bandits" or counter-revolutionaries fled to the mountains after the 1959 Castro Revolution.

Facing the main square is the main church, La Inglesia Parroquial de la Santisima, or easier said in English, The Church of the Holy Trinity, the Trinity being the inspiration for the town's name. Inside is a spectacular carved wooden altar decorated with inlaid wood. What I found of particular interest is one of the side altar pieces. Rarely do you see images of Jesus seated, but here he is depicted seated with his arm bent supporting his head, perhaps contemplating the state of the world.

Also facing the Plaza Mayor is Palacio Brunet, another mansion built by a wealthy sugar family. Today it is known as the Museo Romantico filled with Brunet family treasures.

Alternate transportation in Trinidad.

Inside the Church of the Holy Trinity is this carved wooden side altar showing Jesus in an unusual seated position, perhaps contemplating the state of the world.

And Finally

Here are three phrases that will make your Cuba voyage more enjoyable, if you can just remember them, and internalize their meaning.

"Things change." They do, and especially in Cuba. Cuba is a work in progress. People and policies change. You may think you are going on a certain itinerary, and once you are in Cuba discover that the Cuban government has changed the itinerary and you are not going where you thought you were going. Frustrating? Yes, both for you and the cruise line. But it is what it is. If you are going to visit Cuba, you need to be flexible and have a sense of adventure. This is not a nation with a well-honed tourism where things are predictable. The only predictable thing about Cuba is that it is *not* predictable.

"Travelers" do well in Cuba. "Tourists" often find themselves frustrated. Be a "traveler" and not a "tourist" and you will have an amazing time.

"Approximately." The key phrase to enjoying life and not stressing out in any Latin American country, but especially Cuba. Latins by nature are not as "time driven" as are folks from many other cultures.

Generally, things will happen, but they may not happen as scheduled. As my banker advised me when we first moved to Central America, "Don't stress. Live long." Good advice, although not always easy to follow.

"It's different." Well, that's why you came, isn't it? If you wanted everything the same, you never would have left home. Resist the temptation to always compare Cuba, Cuban life, and the way things are done in Cuba, with the way they are back home. Things aren't "better" or "worse," they are different! And it is exploring the differences that makes life and travel fun and interesting. Absorb the differences. Cubans know their lives are different and you don't have to tell them, or explain how different, better or worse, life is back home where you are from. You are here to explore and to learn. This is a people to people experience where you can share, learn, and appreciate the things that we share and the differences that make our world, and our lives, interesting.

Come with a friendly, positive, open, even humble attitude, and you will have a marvelous adventure.

What were your preconceptions about Cuba, and have there been any changes after your time in Cuba?

In what ways did the reality you experienced differ from expectations that you had before coming to Cuba?

What different perspectives did you hear?

Were you able to chat with any "real" Cubans and what did you learn from them?

Key Dates in Cuban History

- 1492 Columbus arrived in Cuba and claimed the island for Spain
- 1510 Spanish arrived from Hispaniola and the conquest of Cuba began
- 1511 First settlement at Baracoa founded by conquistador Diego Velazquez
- 1512 Hatuey, an Indigenous Cuban resistance leader, was burned at the stake
- 1514 Havana founded
- 1527 First African slaves brought to work in cotton industry
- 1532 and 1537 Slave rebellions crushed
- 1537 – 1578 Repeated attacks by the French
- 1597 Morro Castle constructed to protect Havana harbor
- 1628 Dutch privateer Piet Heyn plundered the Spanish treasure fleet in Havana harbor
- 1649 Epidemic killed a third of the island population
- 1662 English captured Santiago de Cuba
- 1670 In return for Spanish recognition of English ownership of Jamaica, the English left Santiago
- 1741 British captured Guantanamo Bay but withdrew after illness and attack by local guerillas
- 1748 Construction of Havana cathedral completed
- 1748 British and Spanish fleets fought for control in Havana harbor and in Europe
- 1762 British took control of Cuba
- 1763 British ceded Cuba back to Spain in return for Florida under the Treaty of Paris
- 1793 Over 30,000 white refugees fled from Saint Dominique escape the Haitian rebellion and came to Cuba

- 1819 French settlers from Bordeaux and Louisiana founded the first European settlement at Cienfuegos
- 1853 Jose Marti was born in Havana
- 1868 – 1878 Ten Year's War – The first war for Cuban independence from Spain
- 1886 Slavery abolished in Cuba
- 1895 Cuban revolution for freedom from Spain was relaunched
- 1895 Jose Marti killed by Spanish troops in battle
- 1898 Battleship USS MAINE exploded and sank in Havana Harbor killing over 260 crew
- 1898 Treaty of Paris ended the Spanish-Cuban-American War
- 1899 U.S. troops took control of Cuba and appointed governor and government
- 1901 U.S. Platt Amendment stipulated conditions for withdrawal of U.S. troops
- 1902 Cuban Republic established under terms of the U.S. Platt Amendment
- 1903 Treaty of Relations gave the U.S. rights to establish bases in Cuba including at Guantanamo – interpretation and terms remain a point of conflict
- 1906 In midst of chaos U.S. troops reoccupied Cuba
- 1909 U.S. occupation ended
- 1912 Gerardo Machado became dictatorial president
- 1917 Cuba entered WWI on side of Allies
- 1926 Fidel Castro born in province of Holguin
- 1928 Ernesto Guevara [Che] born in Argentina
- 1928 Sergeants' Revolt including Fulgencio Batista toppled provisional government
- 1933 Dictator Gerardo Machado forced out ensuing confusing and violent series of governments controlled by Batista
- 1941 Cuba declared war on Japan, Germany and Italy
- 1943 Soviet Union opened an embassy in Havana

- 1952 Batista supported by army and seized power once more
- 1953 Cuban revolutionaries led by Fidel Castro launched failed attack on Moncada barracks in Santiago de Cuba and Castro captured
- 1954 Batista dissolved parliament and elected president unopposed
- 1955 Batista issued an amnesty to all political prisoners freeing Fidel Castro
- 1956 Castro brothers fled to Mexico where they met Che Guevara
- 1956 Castro and followers, including Che Guevara, Raul Castro and Camilo Cienfuegos, attempted secret return from Mexico on leaky, old yacht Granma and fled to the Sierra Maestra mountains
- 1959 At U.S. urging Batista resigned and fled and Fidel Castro became Premier of Cuba
- 1959 Castro began forming revolutionary government, initiated land reforms, and began seizing properties
- 1960 U.S. President Dwight Eisenhower ordered CIA to train Cuban exiles for a covert invasion of Cuba
- 1960 All U.S. property in Cuba was nationalized
- 1960 U.S. imposed embargo prohibiting all exports except foodstuffs and medical supplies
- 1961 U.S. imposed Trade Embargo on Cuba
- 1961 Failure of U.S. Bay of Pigs Invasion
- 1961 Nikita Khrushchev warned President John F. Kennedy to end U.S. aggression against Cuba
- 1962 Cuban Missile Crisis and U.S. air and sea blockade imposed until Soviets removed offensive weapons from Cuba and U.S. agreed to remove missiles from Turkey and not to invade Cuba
- 1965 Castro allowed Cubans to emigrate launching the Camarioca boatlift and airlift
- 1967 Che Guevara executed on orders of CIA in Bolivia
- 1975 Cuba sent first troops to Africa

- 1980 Cuba allowed up to 125,000 people to depart Cuba by boat from Mariel harbor for the U.S.
- 1983 United States invaded the Grenada and clashed with Cuban troops
- 1991 Soviet Union formally dissolved ending the Soviet support of Cuba
- 1991 Last Cuban troops left Africa
- 1993 Cuba opened state enterprises to private investment
- 1996 Two private planes carrying Cuban Exile leaders were shot down by Cuban fighter jets and U.S. extended the U.S. Embargo against foreign countries
- 1998 Pope John Paul became first Pope to visit Cuba
- 1999 Six-year-old Elian Gonzalez was found clinging to an inner tube in the Straits of Florida
- 2000 Elian Gonzalez was forcibly returned to Cuba
- 2000 Russian President Vladimir Putin visited Cuba
- 2002 Russia's last military base in Cuba was closed
- 2002 Former U.S. President Jimmy Carter visited Cuba and criticized the U.S. Embargo
- 2004 The Cuban government banned transactions in U.S. dollars and imposed a 10% tax on dollar-peso conversions.
- 2005 Hurricane Dennis caused widespread destruction in Cuba and left 16 people dead.
- 2007 Raul Castro assumed duties of President while Fidel Castro recovered from surgeries
- 2008 Fidel Castro resigned as President and was replaced by Raul Castro
- 2012 Pope Benedict visited Cuba
- 2014 U.S. President Barack Obama issued Executive Order opening Cuba to U.S. citizens under a people to people program
- 2014 U.S. President Barack Obama and Cuban President Raúl Castro jointly announced the beginning

of a process of normalizing relations between Cuba and the United States

- 2015 Pope Francis visited Cuba
- 2016 U.S. President Barack Obama visited Cuba
- 2016 Fidel Castro died
- 2017 Donald J Trump became President of the U.S.
- 2017 U.S. Present Donald J Trump replaced the "Obama Executive Order on Cuba" with the "Trump Executive Order on Cuba" – aside from the name change, nothing much changed
- 2017 U.S. President Donald J Trump created more regulations regarding U.S. citizens visiting Cuba, restricting many activities, requiring "approved" supervision, and creating a new level of bureaucracy and paperwork for U.S. citizens visiting Cuba and the sponsoring organizations. U.S. citizens and their paperwork from their visits to Cuba became subject to audit by the U.S. Treasury Department.
- 2018 Cuban President Raul Castro scheduled to retire to senior statesman role

For Further Exploration

"Before Night Falls" (2000) – *Oscar nominated film based on the life of life of Cuban poet and novelist Reynaldo Arenas. Deals with Post Revolution shortages, repression of artists, writers, gays, and the struggle to stay or leave.*

Beltrami, Carla et al, Ed. DK EYEWITNESS TRAVEL GUIDE CUBA. London, Dorling Kindersley, Ltd., 2012. - *I like these DK guidebooks: informative, logical, fabulously illustrated, complete with highlight maps.*

Chomsky, Alvin, Ed. "THE CUBA READER: HISTORY, CULTURE, POLITICS." Durham & London, Duke University Press, 2003. - *It may be a lot to wade through, but if you were taking a college course about Cuba, this would be your assigned reading ... but it's worth the effort. One review says, "What a beautiful journey through five hundred years of Cuban history, culture and politics!" Another says that it "offers a splendid overview of the Cuban experience, past and present, through a dazzling array of points of view."*

"The Cuba Libre Story" (2016) Netflix - *A good eight-part documentary on Cuba. It's very well done ... with one glaring exception, possibly because the movie was financed by the European Union. Netflix has it available in English and Spanish and there are lots and lots of first-person comments, and observations, very good, very international approach, but these are comments mostly in French, German and Spanish. They do have subtitles in English, or whatever language you are watching, but the subtitles are pretty much unreadable! White subtitles on a mostly white background. Incredible! But other than that glaring and frustrating fault, it's a pretty good series.*

Feinberg, Richard E. OPEN FOR BUISNESS: BUILDING THE NEW CUBAN ECONOMY. Washington, DC, Brookings Institution Press, 2016. - *Feinberg has all the academic cred, plus experience at* the U.S. Departments of State and Treasury, to provide a guide to Cuba's movement toward market socialism.

Miller, Tom. TRADING WITH THE ENEMY; A YANKEE TRAVELS THROUGH CASTRO'S CUBA. New York, Basic Books, 1992. - *Miller is an excellent travel writer whose wife is Cuban and so has family in Cuba and has travelled back and forth. He has interesting stories to tell and a unique perspective.*

Staten Clifford L. THE HISTORY OF CUBA. New York, Palgrave Macmillan, 2003. - *A concise, easy to read and understand, summary of Cuban history by a Professor of Political Science at Indiana University.*

"Strawberry and Chocolate" (1993) – *An Oscar nominated film with a cute story line of two friends struggling with shortages and restrictions on intellectuals, gays, and artists in Post Revolution Cuba, wrestling with staying or trying to flee to Miami. An interesting sub-text is the way in which Santeria is a part of daily life.*

Sublette, Ned CUBA AND ITS MUSIC: FROM THE FIRST DRUMS TO THE MAMBO. Chicago, Chicago Review Press, 2004. - *Even if music is not really your thing and you skip over a lot of the musical history, this is a fascinating read, if just for the history and cultural background. I agree with one reviewer who wrote, "If you buy only one book on Cuba in your life, and want the history, culture and politics all in one volume – this is the one." Of course, aside from buying MY book!*

Postscript:

Winslow Homer in Cuba

Winslow Homer (1836–1910) was an American artist known for his pictures of maritime subjects. Born in Boston, he later lived in New York City. He began as a printmaker, then illustrator, and moved on to be a well-known artist who worked both in watercolor and oil.

During the winter of 1884-5 he escaped the cold North East and visited Cuba where he painted a series of watercolors for Century Magazine. The magazine ran from 1881 to 1930, starting out as a religious publication and ending up as the most popular magazine in the country.

Winslow Homer: A Street in Santiago de Cuba 1885

Black and white doesn't begin to convey the vibrancy of these watercolors, but they still breathe the magic that is still Cuba.

RichardDetrich.com

About Richard

Richard Detrich has been hooked on travel since spending three months as a student wandering around Europe on $4 a day.

The next year he worked his way back on the cruise staff of a Dutch student ship and spent another three months, this time traveling more upscale on $5 a day.

Detrich served over thirty years as a pastor, owned cruise only travel agencies in Southern California, was director of e-commerce for a large national fitness company, and sold real estate, the common skill being the ability to communicate. He has an AB, MDiv, MBA and a PhD in nonprofit/church administration.

Richard and his wife both retired early and moved to Panama where they live in the mountains outside of Boquete. His wife's retirement project is growing coffee and Richard's is spending four to six months a year as a Destination Consultant on luxury cruise ships including Princess, Holland America, Celebrity, Crystal, Silversea and Pearl Seas.

When not at sea he enjoys relaxing at home, writing, blogging, gardening, reading in the spa, and spending time with his wife and dogs.

Also Available

THE NEW ESCAPE TO PARADISE tells the story how and why we retired early to Panama: how we sorted through countries, why Panama, and what our lives as expats living in Panama have been like.

If ever you've thought of picking up and moving to a totally new place and culture, here's what you need to keep in mind.

Available on Amazon.

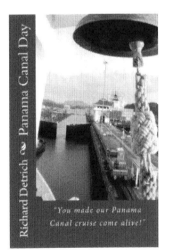

PANAMA CANAL DAY tells the story of Panama and its famous Canal, including all about the new locks and expanded Canal.

Many of the more well-known Canal books focus only on the U.S. period and the construction of the Canal, PANAMA CANAL DAY tells the entire story right up to the present.

Available on Amazon.

Endnotes

[1] This is not intended to be any kind of comprehensive history of Cuba. Rather it is based on hour-long talks designed to summarize highlights of Cuba's history and relationship with the U.S. to familiarize cruise passengers with the basics of Cuba.

[2] According to Richard E. Feinberg, writing in OPEN FOR BUSINESS, "In 2013 the Brazilian government contracted with the Cuban government through the Pan-American Health Organization for the services of some 11,000 – 12,000 Cuban medical professionals, for an annual payment of around $500 million . . . Employing them costs the Brazilian medical service less than it would cost to employ Brazilian doctors, who have avoided practicing in poorer rural districts. In theory, Cuban participants each receive a monthly salary of around $4,500, but in fact they see only $1,245, the difference accruing to the Cuban government."

[3] Christian Pirkl, Creative Commons Share Alike 4.0 International license.

[4] Although I do discuss "Good Neighbors" in my onboard talks, this is greatly expanded content to include more of my own opinions and observations after my visits to Cuba.

[5] Kurt Eichenwald,, "How Donald Trump's Company Violated The United States Embargo Against Cuba," Newsweek, September 29, 2016.

[6] Ibid.

[7] Drew Harwell and Jonathan O'Connell, "With shift on Cuba, Trump could undercut his company's hotel-industry rivals," Washington Post, June 15, 2017

[8] Ibid.

[9] Ibid.

[11] Ibid.

[11] Creative Commons CC0 1.0 Universal Public Domain Dedication

[12] Creative Commons Attribution 2.0 Generic license, spast.hamburg.

[13] Benotzer:Alexandra, GNU Free Documentation License, Version 1.2

[15] Jorge Royan, Creative Commons Attribution-Share Alike 3.0 Unported License

[16] "Evangelical" used here being in the traditional, theological sense of the word, not the "Evangelical" right-wing mostly Republican political context in which it is increasingly used in the U.S. media.

[17] Francesco Gorup de Besanez, Creative Commons Attribution-Share Alike 3.0 Unported License

[18] Photo: Rebecca Detrich

[19] In the U.S. Public Domain

[20] Tom Miller, Trading With The Enemy, New York, Basic Books, 1192, p.202.

[21] Elvert Barnes, Creative Commons Attribution-Share Alike 2.0 Generic License.

[22] Original source thought to originally be CNN.

[23] Piviso.com

[24] Anton Zelenov, Creative Commons Attribution-Share Alike 3.0 Unported

[25] Hectonichus, GNU Free Documentation License, Version 1.2r

[26] Creative Commons Attribution Share-Alike 3.0 License

[27] Friman, GNU Free Documentation License, Version 1.2

[28] Emmanuel Huybrechts, Creative Commons Attribution License Generic 2.0

[29] Jezhotwells, Creative Commons Attribution-Share Alike 3.0 Unported

[30] Anagoria, GNU Free Documentation License, Version 1.2

[31] Joakant, COC 1.1 Universal Public Domain Dedication.